Shad Helmstetter, Ph.D.

Network
of
Champions

What's *Right* About America—
And How To Be A Part Of It!

Chapel
&
Croft
Publishing

Other books by Shad Helmstetter:

What To Say When You Talk To Your Self

The Self-Talk Solution

Choices

Predictive Parenting–
 What To Say When You Talk To Your Kids

Finding The Fountain Of Youth Inside Yourself

Self-Talk For Weight-Loss

You Can Excel In Times Of Change

NETWORK OF CHAMPIONS

Helmstetter, Shad
 Network Of Champions

Printed in USA

10 9 8 7 6 5 4 3

Acknowledgements

There have been many fine individuals who have contributed their time and wisdom to this book. Of these, there have been many Diamonds, and there have been others who I know will be there one day, themselves. Though all of those who so graciously contributed would be too numerous to mention here, and I would not want to omit any of them, I would like to give my heartfelt thanks to each of them:

*You are those individuals who symbolize the kind of caring about others, that makes Amway the exceptional organization it is today. You truly **are** an important part of what is **right** about America!*

This book is dedicated with deepest love and affection to my wife, Bonnie Elise.

Contents

Introduction 1

Part I
The People Who Are Changing
The World 3

Chapter One
The Diamonds In Your Sky 5

Chapter Two
There's More Than Hope, America-
There's Amway 11

Chapter Three
Nine Key Virtues Of
Successful Network Marketing 18

Part II
Getting Past What Stops You 42

Chapter Four
The Difference Between Those Who Succeed-
And Those Who Don't 44

Chapter Five
A Simple Picture Of How It Works 51

Chapter Six
Who's Voting On Your Success? 65

Chapter Seven
A Major Breakthrough In Reprogramming 76

Chapter Eight
Getting Motivated And *Staying* Motivated 89

Chapter Nine
Listening To Self-Talk 102

Part III
Going For It 117

Chapter Ten
10 Snapshots of Network Marketers 119

Chapter Eleven
Overcoming The #1 Problem 138

Chapter Twelve
When Your Family Doesn't Understand 148

Chapter Thirteen
Building Stronger Self-Esteem 165

Part IV
Heading For The Stars 177

Chapter Fourteen
Your Daily Program Checklist 179

Chapter Fifteen
Review, Repeat, and *Reinforce* 190

Chapter Sixteen
Believing In Incredible *You!* 211

Shad Helmstetter, Ph.D.

Network
of
Champions

Introduction

This book was written for individuals and families who are presently Amway Distributors, at any level, regardless of your activity to date. It is also for those people who are thinking about joining the Amway Distributor organization, but are not yet members.

The book has four objectives:

The first is to recognize the importance of the role you play in the Amway Distributor organization, and to recognize the importance of that organization's role in your life and future.

The second is to give you information about the true psychological causes that contribute to your personal success in the business.

The third is to give you the most effective motivational tools I have ever found, to assist you in reaching your goal.

My fourth objective was that the book be easy to read, extremely practical and down-to-earth, and of course, genuinely helpful.

In order to make this the most helpful book possible for you and your organization, I have chosen to write it *specifically* about the Amway organization, rather than about network marketing in general. That way, in each subject we cover, you will know it applies specifically to you.

The book follows a several-year-long study of network marketing organizations, and in particular, the people who are the members of these organizations. This is not a book about the structure of your organization, or your plan, or your presentation. It does not duplicate or replace any of the tools that are already available to you.

Instead, this is a book about the *personal* side of your success—those qualities and characteristics within you that either help you, or hold you back.

Although I have often wished I were a member of your ranks, I have chosen to remain outside any organization, and in so doing, retain my professional status as an external observer and researcher of this field.

It is because of that professional position that I can assure you of the candidness and the objectivity of my observations. What I share with you, about you and your organization, is what I know to be accurate and true.

Most important to me is that this book becomes a companion of yours for years to come. During the past years I have gotten to know many of you. It is my hope that through the pages that follow, we will become fast friends as well.

Here is to your success in Amway. You deserve it.

Shad Helmstetter, Ph.D.

Part I

The People Who Are
Changing The World

"All too often, we stop looking up at the stars.

We forget there are diamonds in the heavens— and one of them is ours."

Chapter One
The Diamonds In Your Sky

*"You are everything that is,
your thoughts, your life, your dreams come true.
You are everything you choose to be.
You are as unlimited as the endless universe."*

With those few words I began my first book, more than a decade ago. What those words tell us is still true today, and it is one of the most important messages of our lives: Your future is unlimited—and it is *up to you.*

Have you ever looked up into the stars on a clear, cool night, and imagined that the sky above you was filled with diamonds?

I remember doing that when I was young. I believed that all I had to do was look up into that incredible universe of diamonds in the heavens above me, find my star, make my wish, and it would come true.

The problem is we get too busy. We stop looking up at those stars. Or we forget *there are diamonds in our own heavens*—and that one of them is ours. The problem is we never quite believe we can have that diamond for ourselves—so we never stand tall enough to reach it.

The problem seems to be in connecting the *dream* that we see in the starlit heavens with the *reality* of down-to-earth, everyday living. "It's all well and good to reach for the stars," you might say, "but I've got a house payment to make, and kids to feed, and *work to do*. I don't have *time* for stargazing; I'm too busy living my life!"

It is my belief that if you're interested in making Amway a part of that life, you probably want something more than what you have now: more time with your family, more freedom to travel, more money . . . at least, that's where involvement with this organization usually *starts*.

Let's take money, as an example. I've talked to a lot of people who started out by joining Amway in order to earn a few hundred dollars extra a month. And that's not a bad idea; if you want to reach financial freedom, if you would like to be numbered among the top 10 or 15 percent of the most financially independent families in the U.S. in the next ten years, there may be no more important organization or opportunity existent today, than the Amway organization. But that's clearly not all there is to it.

IT'S MORE THAN MONEY, OR FREEDOM, OR TIME: IT'S A WAY OF LIFE

Financial freedom is important, of course; when the burden of everyday money worries is lifted, then you can focus on the *other* goals and objectives of a life well lived. Time with your family is one of the most vital objectives you can have. And travel is important, too, to broaden your horizons and take you beyond the limitations you see every day. But it didn't take very many conversations with distributors who had been with the organization for a period of time, for me to confirm what I already knew to be true: that there is much more to Amway than just a financial opportunity, or travel, or even free time.

And the more I watched, and studied, and evaluated your organization, the more convinced I became that even if you joined for one of the reasons I mentioned, you soon became a part of something much bigger and more important. You may have *begun* with a financial need—but you ended up adding to your life by joining Amway, something much richer, both in your life and in the lives of those around you.

WHAT YOU'RE *REALLY* DOING WITH AMWAY

Unless they, too, are in the business, almost none of the people around you have any idea what you're *really* doing, what it could mean to them, or how important you are.

Whether they—or you—are aware of it or not, you are actually in the middle of a very positive "revolution." While you're working the plan, improving your life, and meeting your basic financial goals, you are also changing lifestyles, helping an entire society get back to basic values, reaffirming spiritual beliefs, and turning "success" back over to the people who work for it.

That's a big job, and a more important one than you may have realized. It is work that deserves the best you have to give it, and work that deserves the support of *everyone*, both *inside* and *outside* your organization.

HELPING YOU MAKE IT WORK

If I could sit down and talk with you each day, personally motivating you, teaching you to succeed, I would talk to you as a friend, and someone I believe in.

I would try to get you to see how good you *really* are—not in an immodest or inappropriate way, but in a realistic and practical way.

I would try to show you the truth of what you're really doing as a member of this incredible organization, a truth I can clearly see from my outside vantage point.

I would give you every single tool or truth and technique I could to help you, as someone who wants you to live up to your very best; and it is from that point of view that I have written this book for you.

A MOTIVATIONAL TRAINING "HANDBOOK" FOR AMWAY DISTRIBUTORS

If you're already in Amway, I'm going to share with you some important tools you can use to reach your goals in network marketing. (If you're not yet a member, I hope by the time you finish this book, you are convinced to join.)

In order to share with you the most effective motivational

techniques we've discovered, in this book I've updated and brought together the key concepts from this field for you. I've also organized and focused this research and information and applied it directly to your business. This motivational training "handbook," then, is a summary of the best and most up-to-date motivational tools and concepts—and it is written *specifically for you,* as an Amway Distributor.

It is my goal, by the end of the book, to help you realize how important you and your work in Amway truly are, and to give you all the ammunition and support you need from a *personal, motivational* standpoint to get you where you're going.

You have an incredible opportunity in front of you. I know you have everything it takes within you to make the most of it. I know you can reach the highest star you set your sights on, and that you are able to create the future for yourself and your family, that you see in your dreams—not just in a "stargazing" way, but in the most realistic, practical way there is—so that the next time you look into a starlit night sky, you know you *belong* among those "diamonds," among those sparkling lights.

It is my hope, and my *belief*, that you will one day *become* one of those diamonds in your heavens—and I'm going to do all I can to help you get there.

*"There may be no greater
service you can perform
for the betterment
of your life,
your family,
your community,
your country,
and for the betterment
of mankind . . .*

*Than to be
a positive, active member
of the Amway
organization."*

Chapter Two

There's More Than Hope, America— There's *Amway*

hy do some people succeed in life while others do not? When there is so much opportunity in front of people, why do only a few of them ever reach it and live it out for themselves?

I have spent many years looking for the answers to those questions. I have watched some people grow and achieve, while others fell by the wayside, willing to accept less from themselves, thinking, *"That's just the way life is,"* or contenting themselves to make excuses for dropping out of the race.

In time I found the answers I was looking for. In fact, in my unending quest for the true solutions to success, I was to discover a field of research and a solution that is even now changing the field of personal motivation forever. That field of research, and that discovery, is called "Self-Talk." We learned that by using Self-Talk techniques, people could literally turn lives of failure into lives of growth and success.

It was an important breakthrough, and one that is helping change millions of lives for the better.

But it was during my research that I discovered another success phenomenon—and this one, too, is changing the world.

As I studied and spoke on the positive changes that Self-Talk could create, I found myself in front of audiences in nearly every major city in America. And it was there, in those audiences, that I found the other half of the answer.

WHAT MADE THESE PEOPLE DIFFERENT?

As a behavioral researcher it is my job to study people. So it is not surprising that as I spoke to audiences, and while I was meeting many thousands of people, I began to notice that some of them were *different,* somehow. They were more aware, more interested, more *alive.*

In time I found that I could be introduced to a new audience of several hundred people, and within the first three minutes of my seminar, I could find "them" in the crowd. Even just sitting in the audiences, they looked different. I could see it in their faces. I could see it in their posture—the way they held themselves, the way they sat, the way they leaned forward in their seats, trying to make sure they would soak up every word.

Although a lot of them looked like they had all graduated together from the same "success school," many of them did not know each other, and had never met.

At the end of each of my presentations I would take the time to talk with the attendees. At every opportunity I would talk to these silent achievers and ask them about themselves. They sounded like they did the usual things like have kids in school, go to church, have mortgages, hold jobs, and plan for the future.

But in talking to the "special" people, I began to discover the answer to what made them so much like *each other*, and yet so *different* from everyone *else*. The more of them I talked to, the clearer it became that the one thing almost all of these positive people had in common was that they were all in *network marketing*—and usually, in Amway.

WHY NETWORK MARKETING—AND *YOU*— ARE SO IMPORTANT

During the next few years, I began to explore the beliefs, the attitudes, and the motivations of network marketers in every kind of network company and organization.

I chose to conduct my own independent review of the top organizations. In time, I came to believe that in the life most of us are living right now, *the single, most important inroad to "success" today, is with the Amway organization.*

If that is the case, and I believe that it is, then suddenly the success of network marketing itself becomes very important. Why? Because the success of a community or a nation ultimately depends on the success and well-being of its citizens. It makes sense that the more successful the people are—*individually*—the more successful the community or the nation will become.

It follows, then, that if one of the single strongest forces that lead to the success of the individual today is network marketing, and if Amway is the strongest force in that arena, then it is the Amway organization that could help determine *the very level of success that our nation—and our world—will reach.*

CHANGING YOUR LIFE—
AND CHANGING THE WORLD

When you become a successful Amway Distributor, you are able to literally change your own life in many positive ways. But it doesn't stop there; in fact, that is just where the benefits *begin.*

It is *what you are doing* as you are changing *your* life that makes Amway so important: You are changing your own life by helping other people change *their* lives. And those people help other people change *their* lives. And they, in turn, help other people change *theirs* . . . and so it begins. How many people are there, worldwide, who *could* benefit from becoming an Amway Distributor?

All that is basic knowledge to even the beginning distributor, of course. And yet, in the daily routine of raising kids, paying the rent, and getting to work on time, it is an essential truth that can be all too easily forgotten.

How many professions do you know where you can create positive life changes in *several hundred thousand people* just by talking to—influencing—a few dozen people or a few hundred?

WHAT ABOUT THE ONES WHO *SHOULD* SUCCEED—BUT DON'T?

When I began my study of network marketing organizations, my concern was not their corporate profit, or even the products they marketed. Quality product lines and business profits are certainly important to any good marketing organization. But I was specifically interested in the "people" side of the business; or more accurately put, I wanted to know what happened in the *minds* of network marketers that made them successful.

I wanted to know what happened to those network marketers who were *not* successful. If so many of them can do it, and other members of the same organization do *not*, I reasoned, *then what is stopping the ones who* aren't *making it work?*

Many of the members of the organizations had noticeably more opportunity and more potential within their organization than they were taking advantage of. With the tools they were being given, *almost anyone who had ever seriously considered being successful, could do so.* Yet, these same individuals were often not even working the plan or using the training they received.

It was as though some people were willing to dream for a day or two, or maybe a week or even a few months. And then they would lapse into an old mind set of disbelief.

The result is they would do little or nothing at all with the great opportunity that was in front of them. In the end, they would fail to come close to reaching the rewards they *could* have reached *if they had just worked the plan* that was given to them.

It was obvious that it wasn't Amway's fault, or the fault of the organization. The plan worked; people succeeded with it every day. Something *else* was stopping the ones who hadn't yet made it work.

The more I looked, the more I came to recognize that of the countless individuals who could reach some higher level, only a few of those individuals ever start out by *believing they can do it.*

It was because of this conclusion that I decided to look very closely at what *really* stops some of the members of the most powerful and positive network marketing organization on the planet from succeeding—*when they have already been given everything they need to succeed.*

Let's now take a look at each of the positive steps I've uncovered that can help you make this business work. We're going to begin with the nine key ingredients that are absolutely *essential* to your success.

"This is not the time
to dwell on
your limitations.

This is the time
to stretch your imagination,
expand your horizons,
and get down to the business
of the rest of your life."

Chapter Three

Nine Key Virtues Of
Successful Network Marketing

L et's begin with something that can help your business *immediately*. To do that, we're going to start by looking at some recent discoveries that will help you in the *personal* side of your network marketing business.

I've had the opportunity to look more closely at the motivational behavior side of this business than any writer or researcher I have known. Like a medical doctor examines someone to make sure he is physically strong and healthy, I look, instead, at the strength of people's attitudes, motivations, and self-esteem.

Over the years, I have studied many pathways to "success." Most of those are short-term, like the motivational talks that inspire you for an hour or two, but are gone by the time you wake up the next morning. All that is left is the uncomfortable feeling that you should be doing something different to change your life than you're now doing—but you're not quite sure what it is.

If you would like to follow a success path that lasts, and if you are now an Amway Distributor, you have chosen well. As an objective, outside researcher, I do not believe you will find a better way than following the Amway plan.

Yet there seems to be an underlying sense of doubt in some of the distributors I have met. This doubt comes in the form of a vague discomfort or uneasiness about the *chances* for success. Even with all of the facts in front of you, and even after hearing all of the success stories, that internal discomfort comes back—and it says, *"Can I really make this work?"*

AN IMPORTANT DISCOVERY

In my research, I discovered *why* network marketing, and being an Amway Distributor in particular, is *different* from any other career, business, or job that exists anywhere.

I also discovered the specific reasons *why* people *succeed or fail* in this business—and those reasons are, in several important ways, *unlike* the reasons people succeed or fail in other lines of work.

What I learned was that *successful* distributors have adopted an attitude and style of doing business that is clearly *different*—and I suspect, *superior*—to other businesses. I'm not talking about the steps required to work the plan, or the multi-level structure of the business concept itself.

I'm talking about a set of basic, underlying rules that the

successful distributors apply—and the unsuccessful ones do *not*.

I was able to identify the nine specific requirements—key *virtues*—that you must adopt in order to make your business *work*. Each of these "virtues" was likely taught to you by your sponsors, to some greater or lesser degree of importance, as a normal part of your introduction and training when you became a distributor.

You are probably using several, or maybe even all of these principles already, even if you are not aware they are key virtues. None of them is difficult. In fact, they are the practical, down-to-earth, nuts and bolts of a thriving distributor business.

So when we use the term *virtue* here, we're not talking about some lofty quality that is beyond the reach of the average distributor. Virtues, of the kind we're discussing here, are the kinds of qualities that should have been guiding our lives and our businesses all along.

NINE "KEY VIRTUES"
TO BUILD YOUR BUSINESS

Not surprisingly, your business is the *only* business I found, in which the individual's success is founded on using a combination of *all* nine of these principles. Many businesses use a *few* of them. But no other business seems to embrace and use all nine of them *together*, as they are used by successful distributors.

Even if your goal as a distributor is to do nothing more than make your house payment, or become debt free, or some other, similar starting goal, these same requirements apply. Of course, if your plans include even greater successes than those—as I hope they *do*—adopting these principles will play a *major* role in helping you get there.

Key Virtue #1: *VISION*

Vision is not some high-minded idea. It is basic to your business. And it is *imperative* that you have it.

If someone says to you, *"I don't think I could do this . . . I just can't see it working,"*—that's a lack of vision.

If someone says, *"Look, I've got a job, I'm already doing everything I can to make ends meet . . . there's nothing else I can do . . . "* —that's a lack of vision.

When you hear someone say, *"Maybe some other time . . . "* that's someone whose life is limited to little more than the few small acres of space he walks around in each day.

That is a person who has no vision. That is a person who is preoccupied with "getting by" in a miniature world of his own making. He never takes the time to stop and look *outside* himself—and recognize the truth: *That his life will never be any greater than the dreams he sees in his mind.*

I will never forget one of the times when the importance of having "vision" was brought home to me, in my own life.

Gregory, the youngest of my sons, was only six years old when he and I were discussing his future. We were talking about the incredible life that was in front of him. I was trying to figure out how to show him a picture of his unlimited future, when he, himself, gave me the clue.

While we were talking, he asked me an unusual question for a child of his age.

"How far can I go?" he asked me.

I thought about the depth of that question for a minute or two before an idea came to mind. And instead of giving him an immediate answer in a few, simple words, I got my car keys, and asked Gregory if he'd like to go for a ride.

HOW FAR CAN YOU SEE?

We drove to the highest point on a mountain ridge not far from our home. The sun was setting, and it was a beautiful evening. The clouds that dotted the far horizon seemed to go on and on, into infinity.

After we got out of the car, and were looking off into the far distant vista, I asked him, "How far can you see?"

I'll always remember what my young son said to me as we stood there with that endless evening sky in front of us. He didn't say, "Gee, that's neat." Or, "Can we go home now?"

What he said was, *"I can see forever."*

He was seeing what I was hoping he would see. And it gave me the chance, then, to answer his earlier question. What I said was, "If that's how far you can see, then that's how far you can go."

I don't think that young boy, now a successful young man, ever forgot that important lesson in his life. I know him well. To this day, he believes in the greatest promise of his farthest horizons. He has never lost the vision of his own future.

Even a child of six can understand the basic message. And once you get it, it can last you a lifetime.

HOW IS YOUR VISION RIGHT NOW?
HOW FAR WILL YOU GO?
HOW FAR CAN YOU SEE?

You can only go as far as you can imagine yourself going. If your imagination stops at the office where you work, or at some advancement level a few steps above where you are now—that's exactly how far you will go.

If, on the other hand, your imagination knows no boundaries, *neither will your future.* If you do not allow yourself to have vision, you cannot succeed; you cannot go as far as you could. If you give yourself the gift of vision, you may be able to see "forever." If you ever decide to see forever, and if you ever make the decision to go as far as you can go—I would caution the person or the problem that tries to get in your way.

The virtue of having "vision" is one of the greatest forces of positive energy you can ever add to your life. Without vision, most lives are little more than average. With vision, any life can be great.

What Can You Do, If You Want To Have "Vision?"

Later, I'm going to give you some specific tools that will help you get rid of any limitations you may have placed on yourself in the past. But for now, start by practicing this one on your own. Practice imagining *doing, being,* and *achieving* things you used to think were impossible. If you can't picture yourself achieving your business goals, you'll never get there. So create the *habit,* give it the time it takes, to see your own success in your mind, the way you would most like it to be.

I don't mean this in the way a pep-rally motivator might get you to open up and think differently about your future for a few minutes—and then it goes away. I'm talking about the everyday, down-to-earth practice of creating that future for yourself.

If you're in Amway already, your sponsor and your leaders recommend books to read, tapes to listen to, and group functions to attend. *Follow their advice!* They've already *been* where you are about to go—and they can help. Part of what they're doing is helping you move your own horizons a little farther out. They're helping you practice having *vision*.

Go out with your wife or your husband, or sit down with your sponsor. Set aside an evening reserved solely for the purpose of talking about your future. Don't wait for a birthday, or an anniversary, or for New Year's Day, or for some special event. Do it now. Talk about your potential, your dreams, your wants, and your goals. Take it seriously. Take a pad and pen with you and write notes. What you talk about, and what you write down, is incredibly important. It could change the rest of your life.

You may never find a more important task that you can accomplish in your life, than to see your future as it *ought to be*—and as it *can* be—fix that picture in your mind, and decide to reach that goal.

Key Virtue #2: *POSITIVE USE OF YOUR TIME*

How many times have you heard someone say, *"I just don't have the time right now,"* or *"I'm too busy?"* (How many times have you said it yourself?)

Read those same two success excuses again, but this time, read them as though you were saying them out loud. And this

24

time, I will write those two thoughts as they *really* are. When you say them, this is what you're really saying:

"I don't have the time right now . . . *to be successful.*"

"I'm too busy . . . *for success.*"

That is exactly what people who say "no" to you, about Amway, are *really* saying. And that's also what you're saying to yourself if you're a Distributor, but you can't quite find the time to succeed.

You already have the time management tools available to you through your Franklin Planner and through the training and ideas you get from your sponsor and from your organization.

But the problem here actually has little to do with *time* itself; it has to do with *commitment.* If you have an important goal, nonstop focus, and unswerving commitment—you will find the *time* to succeed. Create the commitment, and you will almost automatically create the time you need to get the job done.

It is because of this truth of human nature, that the next key virtue—*Commitment*—is one of the most important virtues of all. And like all virtues, these two go hand-in-hand.

Key Virtue #3: *COMMITMENT*

Do you own a business right now?

If you are an independent distributor or a network marketer, you own a business. You own a very real business.

Because it's so easy to become involved with the Amway opportunity, some people fail to recognize that it is, first and foremost, a *business*. The result is, they never sit down with their banker, their accountant, their lawyer, or even each other, and make an actual *commitment* to be in business. There is no statement of commitment, no actual contract, real or otherwise, with themselves or with anyone else.

As a number of very successful Diamonds told me, the problem is that the business can just sort of . . . *begin*, without its owners ever recognizing that *this* business is just as important as opening a fast food franchise or a printing store. To my way of thinking, this is *more* important.

IF YOU DON'T *COMMIT*, YOU CAN'T *SUCCEED*

As your sponsor has probably pointed out to you, if you had to go to the bank and get a loan for, say, $100,000, you can be sure you would take your distributor business very seriously. He's right. You would make a commitment.

And if you made that kind of commitment, you would schedule your time and your activities accordingly. (This is why Key Virtue #2: *Time*, which we mentioned previously, is actually created by the right level of commitment.)

If you owned any kind of business that was earning profits of fifty, or *a hundred thousand dollars, or more,* a year, you would consider it a very important business. And yet, if you follow the plan, you are literally gearing up your networking business to do just that.

And it is the commitment to that successful business you need to make now—even if you are just getting started, or if you haven't made any progress yet.

I mention this here because of the number of distributors I have met who haven't done it yet! They haven't really made the commitment. And because of that, *they're not succeeding.*

MAKE A CONTRACT TO COMMIT

If you have not yet made the level of commitment that would truly *guarantee* your success, then this is not a business problem, or a training problem. This is something else. This is your old mental "programs" stopping you from taking the single most important step you must take in order to succeed.

It's not the corporate papers, or the business license, or the letterhead, or the meeting with the banker, or a business contract we're talking about. It is a different kind of contract: a contract between you and yourself, and between you and your spouse. It may not be written on paper, but it is a contract nonetheless. This is a psychological agreement that says, *"I choose to commit. We choose to commit."*

And in creating that contract, the two of you are choosing to *succeed.*

Key Virtue #4: *BELIEF*

There is another reason people stop short of success. This most important reason is called "belief." There are many kinds of belief, but this one is about believing in *you*—and in Amway—and in your future.

First, it's simply a fact that you may not really believe in *yourself.* That's not unusual. Most people question themselves in a lot of situations they encounter, day after day, in their lives. (We're not talking about your spiritual faith here; we're talking about your *ability* to accept yourself as a winner.)

Or, you may not really believe in *"the plan,"* or in Amway, or in "the dream," or in the future that the whole concept of Amway embraces. If you don't have all the belief you need, that, too, is understandable. It's only natural for you to question or doubt something that looks that good. After all, you've seen a lot of good ideas before; why should this one be any different?

CAN YOU REALLY BELIEVE IN YOUR FUTURE WHEN YOU HAVEN'T *SEEN* IT YET?

There is one kind of belief that is a form of faith. You just "believe." But the kind of belief we're talking about here is actually a *skill*; it is something you *learn* how to do; it is a virtue you *practice.*

I was surprised at the number of super-sharp Diamonds, among others, who told me that of all of the Amway members they knew, few of those Distributors knew how important they were—and what they were really accomplishing—*until after they had already been there.*

That is, almost no one I interviewed had any real idea of the *true* importance of his or her "role" in the success of literally *thousands* of other people, until long after their own success had already been achieved.

For years, as I studied the organization, and the people that formed its ranks, I was impressed by the attitudes of even the first-year Amway entry-level enthusiasts. Almost everyone I met who was with Amway seemed to have caught at least a part of some very incredible dream. The more I studied, and researched, and interviewed, the more I came to believe that these people had become a part of something very special.

What I did *not* know was that many of the people I was admiring and respecting had no *idea* they were special in any way.

What Can You Do To Create More Belief?

If you'd like to believe in yourself, more than ever before, and if you'd like to have so much belief in what you're doing that it cannot possibly fail—I encourage you to make the *choice* to *practice* the virtue of believing. The more you *practice* this virtue, the more natural your belief will become.

YOU CAN MAKE THE *DECISION* TO BELIEVE

If you would like to be successful, but you are unsure—either about Amway, or about yourself—make the decision to believe! For now, put every disbelief you have aside. Don't try to analyze, don't try to disagree, don't criticize, don't condemn, and don't fight for some reason to stop it or put it off.

What we are trying to do here is to keep *anything*, especially *you*, from getting in the way of your success.

The Amway plan and concept have worked for tens of thousands of other people who had a whole lot less to offer than you. They have built new homes, sent their kids to college, put more money in the bank than they will ever need, increased their faith, and literally created new lives for themselves, *just because they made the decision to believe, follow the plan, and let the Lord provide.*

It didn't take growing up in the right kind of family, going to the right kind of college or getting a special degree; it didn't take government assistance, or some kind of luck.

It took making the *choice* to believe.

If you don't quite believe yet, make a deal with yourself to believe for just one year. Or for six months.

If you add the virtue of belief to your life and to your business, and follow the plan—in not too long a time you will be one of those who have already *done* it. And you will be telling someone else, "For now . . . just *make the decision to believe* . . . and keep working the plan."

Key Virtue #5: *SELF-ACCEPTANCE*

Let's settle this one right away:

There is no wrong personality for Amway.

Of course it helps if you are positive, and confident, and motivated; those kinds of skills help you win at *anything* you do. But those are *skills.* Having a positive attitude, having confidence, being motivated—those are not personality traits you were *born* with; you *learn* them.

If you thought for a *moment* that you didn't have the right personality for Amway, I would show you an unlimited number of people *just like you* who have already succeeded.

There is a great myth that would have us believe it takes a

certain "type" of a person to be good at presenting ideas (that's called "selling"). *It's not true.* Some of the most persuasive people I have ever known are the quietest, or the most analytical; some of them even worry about being shy.

But they are top professionals because they believe in what they are offering, and they take the time to perfect their presentations.

NO ONE WAS "BORN" A DIAMOND

In reviewing the many Diamonds I have interviewed, as impressive as they are today, I doubt there is a single one of them who would say he was "born" with every quality it took to succeed. Any one of them might have been told, *"I don't think you're cut out for this."* (I know for a fact that at one time, many of them believed that themselves.)

How Do You Get The Right Personality?

Don't worry about having the right personality. Don't ever think you're not a winner just because you don't have every skill you'd like, or because you believe you're not lucky enough, or you don't have the background it takes, or you've failed in the past, or you haven't succeeded fast enough.

I'm not suggesting you shouldn't improve yourself. I believe we should work to improve ourselves until there is no breath left in us. Getting better is part of what a life with purpose is all about.

But who you are *right now* is someone who is perfectly

capable of doing well. Of course you can get better, but if you would like to make this business work, you should know this:

It is not your "personality" that counts the most.
It is not your past.
It is not your education.
It is not your background.
It is not your family.

It is *you*.

You're what counts. You . . . *right now, just as you are.* You are much more than the personality you carry around with you—the part that other people see. (That's only a *part* of your identity—and not always the most *accurate* part.) With what *you* have right now, inside—the *real* you—you can acquire the rest of what you need.

All of the "working tools" you need, you already have. If you have old mental programs that you need to change, you can change them. But for now, you should know that there has never been a more "right" personality that yours.

Skills you can work on. *Programs* you can change. But *you* are just fine.

Key Virtue #6: *TAKING RESPONSIBILITY FOR YOURSELF*

Throughout the ages, people who have wanted to *rise above the average,* have been haunted by the same kinds of doubts as those which would try to stop you now.

Maybe your wife or your husband doesn't like the idea of

joining Amway, or your boss thinks you're crazy, or some relative thinks it's a waste of time, or your best friend tells you he knows "all about Amway" and tries to convince you it can't really work.

NO ONE HAS THE RIGHT TO STAND IN YOUR WAY

I have never met *anyone*, who really knew *anything* about Amway, who said it wouldn't work. If someone says, "Don't do it," you can be certain that person does *not* know what he is trying to convince you he knows. That's just someone who is trying to appear to be knowledgeable when, in fact, that person has no knowledge at all.

Those are people who are trying to reshape their ignorance into a false facade of personal importance. Those are also the same people who try to tell you *not* to do something that could earn you $20,000 a *month*, when they are struggling to earn $20,000 a *year*.

The problem is, all of those people are *wrong*—but they're in a position to try to influence you. If you let them, they can talk you out of your dreams.

If only they *knew!* If only they had any *idea* what they were missing! More people who *could* become Diamonds, or Emeralds, or Rubies, *stop*—even before they become Direct Distributors. They don't stop because they can't *make* it; they fail because they give in to the negative beliefs of *others*.

When you have to overcome opposition from other people, before you can get started for yourself, it can take so much energy that you might wonder whether it's worth it to even try.

But the answer to this problem doesn't really have anything to do with anyone else.

The solution has to do with *you.*

I once pointed out that the only person who ought to have the right to do any of your thinking *for* you, was the person who was willing to be *buried* with you—on the same day. (Very few people you will ever meet would be willing to do that.)

You are ultimately, and every day, responsible for yourself. That is part of your contract with your future. You have to be willing to exercise your right to independence on this one. That doesn't mean you don't love or care about the people around you. It simply means that no one else can help you take responsibility for yourself.

If you would like to live, and grow, and achieve, and succeed, especially now, through Amway, then *no one has the right to make that decision for you—*or to *stop* you.

IF YOU HAD THE *NEXT* FIVE YEARS TO LIVE OVER AGAIN . . .

Instead of listening to the negativity of others, listen to the voice of your own *future.* If another you, a much older, wiser you, were to visit you now, and tell you what to do—what would that other you tell you to do?

We are so used to looking back at the last five or so years, and saying, "If I had it to live over again, I would do it differently this time!"

There is a far more important question for you to ask yourself. That question is: "If you had the *next* five years to live over again, what would you do differently this time?"

The point is, you *do* have the next five years to live. And the next *ten*, and the next *twenty*. What would you do with those years—if you *could*?

What would you do next? What would you do every day during that time—so that when you got there, you would not have to say, "If I could live that time over again, I would do it differently this time"?

If you want to get past the negatives, and the questions, and the doubts, and the opposition from others, you will have to do that within yourself. You will have to make a deal with yourself to overlook the negatives, and get on with your life. No one else can do that for you.

You can decide to listen to others and care about others. You can decide to persuade others to *join* in your *success!* But that success, if you're going to really earn it, has to be a choice that *you* decide to make.

There may be some people who try to talk you out of creating a real Amway business. They may not believe that you can ascend to heights they cannot even imagine for themselves. Don't listen to them. *They are wrong.*

There may be other, very important people whom you have chosen to make a part of your life: your wife, or husband, or other members of your family.

But when it really gets down to it, *your future, and what you do with it, is up to you.* You can share your life with others, but you will have to vote for yourself. That is the basis of personal responsibility. And that is the beginning of success in Amway.

Key Virtue #7: *CARING ABOUT OTHERS*

This is a business that is founded on wanting to see other people do better—and a genuine willingness to help them succeed.

As we all know, people who are in this business just to take care of themselves, for a quick, personal reward, don't do well here. But fortunately, the business itself attracts people who care about people. So most of the people you meet in your organization (those who remain, and prosper), will almost always be those who do not have to be convinced to care about others—it comes naturally to them.

And yet, if you make certain that *caring* is a virtue—one that you practice consciously—your caring will go further, and it will be stronger. It is the difference between "kind of caring," passively, and *"caring about caring"*—actively.

For years, each time I have stood in front of an audience, preparing to speak, I have always paused for a moment to place in my mind the thought that an old friend gave me many years ago.

"Before you speak," my friend told me, "look out over the audience, and imagine that each of those people is actually attending your family reunion—and all of them sitting there are actually your family and friends. And then imagine that this is the last time you will be able to speak to them, ever again. What would you say to them, then?"

My old friend probably never knew how much he had given to my life by telling me that. Throughout these years, though I have stood in front of thousands of people in audiences everywhere, I have never once, yet, felt the slightest moment of fear or doubt. How could I? I have been talking to my friends.

I believe the same caring is true whether you are talking to a thousand people, or a dozen, or a couple sitting across from you in your living room. If you care about them, it shows.

You may care already, but since caring is a virtue, it is something that can be *practiced*, and even improved. Practice this virtue every chance you get. (Today would be a good day to practice.) When you do, notice how much more you begin to see into that other person's life.

It is there you will find the wants, and the dreams, and the fears, and the hopes—and the needs you have come to fulfill.

People who don't genuinely care about others miss that. People who *care*, always find more opportunity to *share*.

And that is what your business is all about.

Key Virtue #8: *SPIRITUAL VALUES*

For many successful people, this is the first, and the most important key virtue of all. And I agree that bringing your spiritual values and strength into every area of your life, including your business, can have a profound effect on how well you do, and who you grow into as a successful person.

Throughout the years I have been inspired by many people. But I have observed that I have never been inspired by *anyone* who did not have *spirit* within him, or for whom God had no place in his life. Why is that?

The word "*inspire*" means to *put spirit within*. If you do not have the spirit within you, how can you inspire—*give spirit to*—someone else?

When I speak or conduct an hour or two of motivational Self-Talk training at one of the large Amway weekend functions, whenever possible my wife and I try to stay over to attend that other special event that takes place on Sunday morning. Why do we and so many others find it so fulfilling? It is because it replenishes our spirit!

The world you and I are living in right now, especially the media—radio, newspapers, and in particular, television—works against all of our best efforts to live a spiritual life. So much of what we see and hear tries to take our spiritual energies from us! Adding spiritual values to your life every day replenishes the soul, and gives back what the rest of the world is trying to take away.

It's a good idea to make sure you're there on Sunday morning at the next function you attend. But don't just wait for the next rally or function. Don't forget the other Sundays in between—and the Mondays and Tuesdays, and Wednesdays and the rest of the days of the week.

People who have—and _practice_ having—strong spiritual values in their lives are always the people who have more _meaning_ in their lives—more _value_ in every other area. Underlying everything they do, there is a _purpose_, a reason for being that transcends the day-to-day living in the material world around them.

Without that sense of a higher purpose, people end up doing little more than living a life of trying to blot out the unconscious foreboding of hopelessness: the empty feeling inside that says all is not well—but they're not quite sure what it is that's missing.

The person who consciously works to add strong spiritual values to _everything_ he does—and that includes his business—is a person who finds balance and inner strength. The person who is rich in spirit will always have more riches than material wealth. He is the person who finds more meaning in _everything_ he does, and finds _true_ happiness in the rewards.

I am not, in any way, suggesting to you what your religious or spiritual beliefs should be. I would never do that; what you choose to believe is personal, and should remain entirely up to you. But I *am* suggesting you make your spiritual values a strong part of every moment, every day.

Key Virtue #9: *POSITIVE REPROGRAMMING*

Having the wrong mental programming is the greatest reason of all why people fail—at *anything*. And it is certainly a key reason why people fail in network marketing. I've chosen to leave this virtue until last because it is the *basis* of all the other elements you need to succeed.

Without the right programming, none of the other ingredients of successful network marketing can work for you on a long-term basis. If you have the wrong *programs*, you will continually sabotage yourself, without even quite knowing why.

We'll give the solution to this problem an in-depth look in the following chapters. To help you change old mental programs, I will also give you some word-for-word suggestions for building *new* programs—with some of the exact programming messages you need to help you excel as an Amway Distributor.

ARE YOU WILLING TO MAKE IT WORK?

If you build those nine principal virtues into your business, and into your life, you will greatly increase your chances for success. None of those virtues is impossible—or even difficult to adopt. But all of them, practiced together, are *essential* to true success.

You *could* just work the plan, of course. And if you kept doing that, you would reach a certain level of success. You may even be able to do that—for a time—*without* building your business on the kinds of virtues we have been discussing. You most certainly could make the extra income, probably make the house and car payment, and maybe even go a step or two beyond where you are now.

But *real* success, the lasting kind, is more than that. It will help you to keep the following list of questions handy, in order to remind yourself of the importance of the key principles we've discussed in this chapter.

1. Are you willing to *see your future* without limitations?

2. Are you willing to *spend your time* being successful?

3. Are you willing to *commit* to owning a real business?

4. Are you willing to make the decision to *believe*?

5. Are you willing to recognize your *personality* is fine?

6. Are you willing to take *responsibility* for yourself?

7. Are you willing to genuinely *care about others*?

8. Are you willing to bring the *spiritual values* that are important to you into every area of your life?

9. Are you willing to *change the programs* that have stood in your way?

If you'd like to *enjoy* your success while you're reaching it, and hold on to that success throughout your life, make those nine essential virtues—and others like them—a part of everything you do.

Memorize them. Write them down. Reread them regularly. Bring them up at the breakfast table, discuss them with your spouse, and make them a conscious part of every day. They will help you reach every worthwhile goal you set. And they will be counted among your best companions along the way.

IT'S TIME TO GET PAST THE OLD PROGRAMS

Now let's look more closely at Key Virtue #9, *Positive Reprogramming*, the element that is behind anyone's success—in *anything*. Our objective is to find out how we can get past the barriers of old programs that have been standing between you and your own success.

In order to do that, we will take a fascinating look at how your programming *really* works.

Part II
Getting Past What Stops You

"The difference between
those who do it
and those who don't . . .

Is that those who do it,
do it—
And those who don't,
don't."

Chapter Four

The Difference Between Those Who Succeed—And Those Who Don't

I n order to reach your dreams (or get anywhere worthwhile), it is a good idea to first get rid of any stones or weights that may be holding you back. Without a doubt, the most important weights we carry with us are our old programs.

I once wrote a parable about the importance of "programming" in our lives. The story is about an old man and a boy. It is a simple parable that in some ways could be about any of us.

THE STORY OF SARTEBUS AND KIM

There is a story of an old man and a young boy who lived in ancient times. The old man was named

Sartebus, and the boy was named Kim. Kim was an orphan, living on his own, making his way from village to village in search of food and a roof over his head. But most important of all, even more than his search for a full stomach and a comfortable dry place to sleep, Kim was looking for something else—he was searching for a *reason*.

"Why," he wondered, "do we travel throughout our lives in search of something we cannot find? Why must things be as difficult as they are? Do we make them so ourselves, or is it just meant to be that we should struggle as we do?"

These were wise thoughts for a boy as young as Kim, but it was just that kind of thinking that caused him to find along the way an old man, traveling the same road, who, Kim thought, might help him with an answer or two.

The old man was carrying on his back a large, covered, woven basket that appeared to be very heavy, especially for someone as old and weary as he was. When they stopped to rest beside a small brook along the road, the old man wearily settled his basket on the ground. To Kim it looked as though the man carried all of his worldly goods in that one basket; it seemed to be much heavier than even a much younger, stronger man could carry very far.

"What is it in your basket that makes it so heavy?" Kim asked Sartebus. "I would be happy to carry it for you. After all, I am young and strong, and you are old and tired."

"It is nothing you could carry for me," answered the old man. "This is something I must carry for myself."

45

And he added, "One day, you will walk your own road and carry a basket as weighted as mine."

Over many days and many roads, Kim and the old man walked many miles together. And although Kim often asked old Sartebus questions about why men must toil as they do, Kim did not learn from him any of the answers, nor could he learn, try as he might, what treasure of such great weight was in the basket the old man carried.

Sometimes late at night, at the end of a long day's journey, Kim would lie quietly, pretending to sleep, listening to the old man sorting through the contents of his basket by the flickering light from a small fire, and talking quietly to himself. But in the morning, as always, he would say nothing.

It was only when Sartebus could walk no more, and he lay down to rest for the last time, that he told young Kim his secret. In their last few hours together, he gave to Kim not only the answer to the riddle of the basket he carried, but the answer to why men toil as they do.

"In this basket," Sartebus said, "are all of the things I believed about myself which were not true. They are the stones that weighted down my journey. On my back I have carried the weight of every pebble of doubt, every grain of the sand of uncertainty, and every millstone of misdirection I have collected along my way. Without these I could have gone so far. I could have lived a life of the dreams I saw in my mind. But with them I have ended up here, at the end of my journey." And without even unwrapping the braided cords that bound the basket to him, the old man closed his eyes and quietly went to sleep for the last time.

Before Kim himself went to sleep that night, he untied each cord that bound the basket to the old man and, lifting it free, carefully set it on the ground. When he had done this, he just as carefully untied the leather straps that held the woven cover in place, and lifted it aside. Perhaps because he had been looking for an answer to his own question, he was not at all surprised at what he found inside. The basket, which had weighted old Sartebus down for so long, was empty.

THE PROGRAMS THAT STOP YOU

How many of us fail because we go through life carrying our fears and our limitations in a basket on our backs?

We already know most of our fears are self-created—but they seem so real we could almost reach out and touch them. We even admit that most limitations are "imaginary"; at least that's what we say when we're talking about someone *else's* limitations. Yet our fears and our self-imposed limitations can be so strong they literally stop us from coming close to what we could have achieved—if only we could find a way to stop carrying that basket around with us.

As we now know, those fears and limitations are real—at least they are real in the brain. And we now know the correct term for those mental fears and limitations: they are called *"programs."* And it is those programs that will determine how successful you will become as a network marketer.

Read the following list of just a few of the questions that sometimes frustrate even the most enthusiastic distributors:

What stops you from picking up the telephone and making that call?

Why is it easy to put off doing something that you know needs to be done?

Why can people say they are going to get moving, take action and make contacts, and then not do it?

Why can you feel motivated after an exciting weekend rally or after a rousing motivational speech—and then go back to feeling unmotivated again, just days—or even hours—later?

Why do so many distributors wish they could be successful, but never believe they will be?

Why will one person in a family think that becoming a distributor is a great idea—and then the wife or husband will try to shoot the idea down, or say it will never work?

Why are some people negative, critical, or down on the world?

What causes fear? What makes people stop doing what they know they should be doing?

Why do people think that someone else might be able to succeed, but they themselves, will not?

Why do some people never become Rubies, or Emeralds, or Diamonds . . . when they truly want to succeed, and they have everything they need to do it?

YOUR SUCCESS IN *ANYTHING* YOU DO
IS DETERMINED BY YOUR PROGRAMS

Those are similar to the kinds of questions that have plagued leaders and managers for years. And there is only one answer that applies to all of them: *Our success in anything we do, is always determined by the programs we carry with us.*

Like Sartebus, the old man in the story, all of us have programs, and few of us ever stop long enough to examine what is in the basket—much less take the basket of limitations off, lay it down, and get rid of it for good.

So, what are these ever-present programs that are so powerful they can stop you in your tracks, or make you doubt your own strength, or cause you to hold back, or maybe never let you succeed at all? Where do these programs come from? And is there anything we can do about them? Let's find out.

"The 'programs' you carry
with you, right now,
will always determine
how successful you will be
in anything you do.

Your programs
make the difference
between being a success—
and anything less."

Chapter Five
A Simple Picture Of How It Works

I f you are already involved in the life-changing world of Amway, or if you are even thinking about changing your future by joining the team, you can be assured that you already have some programs that are working for you. It has been my experience that a positive organization such as Amway automatically attracts people who already have some very positive programs. When it comes to programs, "like always attracts like."

But *your* success in *anything* you do is going to depend on you having the *greatest* number of good programs you can get. You already have a good start—and that's good news—but imagine what you could do if you had all of the right programs working for you right now.

Making sure you can replace the *wrong* programs with the exact *right* programs should be one of your most important goals. Helping you do that is one of the primary objectives of this book.

First, it will help you to know, briefly, how the programming process works. To do that, I will take a very complex field of research and *over*simplify it.

I will summarize ten or fifteen years of intense and ground-breaking research in the fields of neurology and molecular biology, and in a few short paragraphs, I'll do my best to show you what the researchers have discovered. If you stay with me for the next few pages, an easy chapter or two of this book, you'll know more about what holds you back—and how to get *past* it—than most people around you will ever discover.

Recently, the people whose job it is to study the human brain have learned more about *why* we do what we do, than was known throughout all of history before that time. What they have learned has unlocked some very important secrets that have to do with your success as an Amway Distributor.

As you will see, these recent discoveries are directly helping people who want to be highly *motivated* and highly *successful*—in short, this is great stuff for network marketers. Because it will help you to understand what they have learned, I'll give you a brief overview of the discoveries they've made.

In its simplest form, here's what we have learned.

YOUR *"MENTAL COMPUTER"* CONTROLS YOUR SUCCESS IN NETWORK MARKETING

Most of the recent breakthroughs in mind/brain research have been made possible by new computer technology. The new "medical imaging technology" allows researchers, for the first time, to look into the human brain *while it is operating.* Now they can watch us think, *while we're thinking*—and a whole lot more.

The researchers found that in many ways, your brain operates much like a powerful, personal computer. There are differences, of course, but in many respects, even the most powerful computers we have today are patterned after the *human* computers that created them.

Many of the functions of the brain can be compared to specific parts and functions of a computer. Most computers have keyboards, video screens, and floppy disks. We have learned that you and I have similar parts. Here are a few of the computer-like parts that *you* have that help you get through each day.

YOUR COMPUTER "KEYBOARD"—
YOUR FIVE SENSES

You were born with your own personal computer keyboard. On a computer, the keyboard is what we use to type in new messages or commands—or anything we want to "program" into the computer. In us, the computer keyboard is our five senses. It is through our five senses that we get all of the messages that are programmed into us.

Imagine that you were born holding your keyboard out to the world in front of you. If you could have said anything, you might have sounded like this:

"Here, Mom; here, Dad; here, world—I don't know how to

do this yet, so I need some help typing in my programs. Would you please type in who I am, and what direction I should go? That's the direction I will follow. Along the way, I need you to type in some values, and some strength, and some courage and some integrity, so I'll be able to stay on the path you set for me.

"But most of all, along with the life you have given me and the love you will share with me along the way, I need you to tell me how far I will go . . . and that's exactly how far I'll go, and what I'll do, with this life in front of me. *Please, would you program me so that I can live up to my full potential . . .* would you show me who I *can* become?"

But our parents, and our teachers, and our brothers and sisters, and all the other people around us did not know that on top of our keyboard was a bright yellow diamond-shaped sign that said, *"Warning! Anything you type into this child's computer keyboard will be stored for life—and acted on as though it is true."* They didn't know; if they had known, they would never have given us most of the programs they gave us.

Look at what we've discovered about our own "mental computers" and the programs *you* have been receiving:

Since the moment you were born, every message you have ever received has been programmed into your personal computer—and stored permanently in your brain.

That means that *every* message you have ever received—everything that has ever been said to you, everything you've ever seen or experienced, everything you've ever done, everything you've ever said, everything you've thought consciously, and even those thoughts you didn't know you were thinking—*every single message you have ever gotten, from any source, has been programmed into your brain, and stored there permanently.*

THE COMPUTER STORAGE CENTER— YOUR SUBCONSCIOUS MIND

The researchers have also learned that when you were born you received a "floppy disk," like the magnetic disk used to record new programs or information in computers. In your computer brain, however, that storage disk is called your "subconscious mind."

We've also learned that the subconscious mind follows specific *rules*—and these rules are important to the programs that affect your success in network marketing right now:

Rule 1. Every program you have ever received—from any source—has been stored permanently in your subconscious mind.

Rule 2. The subconscious mind—that part of the brain that stores the programs—does not know the difference between something that's TRUE and something that's FALSE.

Could you walk up to your computer keyboard at home or at the office and type something into it that's not *true*? Yes, of course you could. Would your computer care? Of course not! (Otherwise we couldn't write novels.)

Your computer just accepts and stores anything you program into it—and your subconscious mind does the same thing, because that's what it was designed to do.

Rule 3. The subconscious mind is designed to always act on the strongest *programs it has.*

The programs *you* have right now that are strongest are the programs that are in control. You don't even have to know what programs they are, or where they came from.

Rule 4. The subconscious mind is designed to get more of (or duplicate) the programs it already has that are the strongest.

Whatever programs you already have, you consciously and *unconsciously* seek out or attract more programs just like them. Instead of working to get rid of programs that are working against us, we *copy* them.

HOW OFTEN WERE YOU TOLD WHAT YOU COULD *NOT* DO?

In my first book about Self-Talk, I included the estimate that during the first 18 years of life, the average person is told *"no,"* or what he or she *cannot* do, more than *148,000* times.

I'm now convinced that's a *low* estimate. A lot of the messages we got while we were growing up were never even said to us out loud! What about "that look" we got at the dinner table? Or how about the test papers that came back from the teacher with the number *wrong* on top instead of the number *right*? Or the parent who didn't show up for some event he or she should have attended?

We got hundreds of thousands of messages, both spoken and unspoken. However many programs we received, we don't have to look too closely to know many of those programs were the wrong kind.

The question here isn't whether you or I got a hundred thousand programs like those, or a half a million. The truth is that *all* the programs you received, regardless what they were, are still with you today, and the programs that are strongest—in you—are the programs in control right now.

77% OF ALL OUR PROGRAMS MAY BE FALSE

According to behavioral researchers, *as much as 77% of all our programs are false.* That means that as much as *three-fourths* of all our programs may be *wrong*, counterproductive, or working against us. And that's if we grew up in a reasonably positive home! What if that estimate is correct?

With some people I've met, it seems that as much as ninety or ninety-five percent of their programs are working against them! All you have to do is look at them in their endless struggles: fighting their way through a life filled with problems, following a path so poorly laid that they literally have no idea where they're headed. That's a life that isn't working. That's a person whose programs have failed.

Fortunately, most of us have been blessed with some better programs than that. But what about the programs we have that *are* the wrong kind?

I once suggested to my readers that they compare those programs to the programs that are typed into the onboard computer on an airplane.

Let's say I invited you on an all-expenses-paid tropical vacation for two weeks in St. Thomas. The great day comes, and we're at the airport, excited and ready to go. They announce our flight, and we gather our bags with our suntan lotion and snorkels and paperback books, and begin to board the plane. But just as we are getting on the plane, we hear the navigator whispering to the captain—and he says, "Captain, we have a *problem!*"

The captain says, "What's that?" and the navigator tells him—and *us*: "Captain, we've just found out that *77%* of the airplane's onboard computer programs—*the programs that fly the plane*—are the *wrong* programs!"

If we overheard that bit of news, what would we do next?

We would get off the plane—as fast as we could go! If 77% of that airplane's onboard computer programs are the wrong programs, that plane is going to *crash*—or land in entirely the wrong place. Those are the programs that determine that airplane's *course, altitude, speed,* and final *destination*—*everything* about the trip we are about to take.

THE PROGRAMS SETTING *YOUR* COURSE AND DIRECTION RIGHT NOW

You might say, "But my programs are better than that. I don't have 77% of my life's programs that are the wrong kind."

I hope you're right. But would you get on that airplane if you heard that only *50%* of its programs were the wrong programs? No, you wouldn't. What about *25%*?

I would not get on that airplane, nor would you get on it with me, if we heard that *any* of its programs were the wrong programs.

And yet we do it every day! We get up in the morning, put our computer disk in, and take off into our day. Imagine being able to hold in your hand a floppy disk that contained every single program you have right now. Now imagine tucking that disk under your arm each morning and having it begin *programming* and setting up your day for you.

Instantly, the programs start to play . . . *Should I really work the plan today? . . . No, I'll put that off until next week . . . Get organized? . . . A little later, maybe . . . Attend the Free Enterprise weekend coming up? . . . Maybe next time . . . Have a great day? . . . No, it's another rotten Monday . . . Get my task list done today? . . . Take charge and get in control? . . . I just don't feel up to it . . . !*

I'm not implying that your programs are anything like those. Your day may always get off on the right foot and stay that way. But however it goes, whatever you do—today and *every* day—you can be sure the programs you carry with you determine *your* course, altitude, speed, and destination.

Your programs determine what you think and do about anything and everything, every moment. Just like with the airplane, your programs make the difference between a life that's not working quite right, and one that could be working a whole lot better—the essential difference between a Diamond and a "dropout."

THE RETURN OF THE "HOT 100"

I have often shared with my audiences my list of 100 of the most typically "negative" Self-Talk phrases I've collected from people over the years. I call the list my "Hot 100." Notice how many of the seemingly "harmless" Self-Talk phrases show us deeper programs that reflect attitudes and habits which tie in with not being fully in control of our lives. In reality, none of these Self-Talk phrases is *harmless* at all.

If you've ever had the chance to read this list before, read it now as the person who wants to succeed in Amway, and wants to let *nothing* get in the way.

As you read, see if you know anyone who says something similar, or if you have said something like any of these yourself:

I can't remember names.
It's going to be another one of those days!
It's just no use!
I just know it won't work!
Nothing ever goes right for me.
That's just my luck.
I'm so clumsy.
I don't have the talent.
I'm just not creative.
Everything I eat goes right to my waist.
I can't seem to get organized.
Today just isn't my day!
I can never afford the things I want.
I already know I won't like it.
No matter what I do, I can't seem to lose weight.

I never have enough time.
I just don't have the patience for that.
That really makes me mad!
Another blue Monday!
When will I ever learn?
I get sick just thinking about it.
Sometimes I just hate myself.
I'm just no good!
I'm too shy.
I never know what to say.
With my luck I don't have a chance!
I'd like to stop smoking but I can't seem to quit.
Things just aren't working out right for me.
I don't have the energy I used to.
I'm really out of shape.
I never have any money left over at the end of the month.
Why should I try—it's not going to work anyway!
I've never been any good at that.
My desk is always a mess!
The only kind of luck I have is bad luck!
I never win anything!
I feel like I'm over the hill.
Someone always beats me to it!
Nobody likes me.
I never get a break!
It seems like I'm always broke!
Everything I touch turns to "bleep."
Nobody wants to pay me what I'm worth.
Sometimes I wish I'd never been born!
I'm just no good at math.
I lose weight, but then I gain it right back again.
I get so depressed!

I just can't seem to get anything done!
Nothing seems to go right for me!
I'm just not a salesperson.
That's impossible!
There's just no way!
I always freeze up in front of a group.
I'm nothing without my first cup of coffee in the morning.
I just can't get with it today.
I'll never get it right!
I just can't take it anymore!
I hate my job.
I get a cold this time every year.
I'm really at the end of my rope.
You can't trust anyone anymore!
I just can't handle this!
I never seem to get anyplace on time.
I've always been bad with words.
If only I were smarter.
If only I were taller.
If only I had more time.
If only I had more money.
If only I were thinner . . .
. . . and on, and on, and on.

And those kinds of programs are just a brief glimpse of the deeper programs that lie below the surface! Imagine sitting down at your personal computer keyboard and typing any one of those directions into the computer, knowing that our Self-Talk actually gets programmed *physically* in our brains!

And now imagine that your computer will do whatever you program it to do—because *it will.*

It's no *wonder* we fail to get where we are trying to go in our lives when we take a look at some of the strong programs we've been living with!

The rule is:

*The **strongest** program always wins.*

That means when any question comes up that has to do with your success, like *"Do I make this call, or do I put it off until tomorrow?"* what you do next will be the result of the programs you have that are the strongest.

Now let's examine where your programs "live," and how they help you determine what you'll do next.

*"Imagine what you could do
if every single program you had
was exactly the <u>right</u> program . . .*

*Success would be
a lot easier to reach.*

*And it would probably take you
a lot less time to get there."*

Chapter Six

Who's Voting On Your Success?

I magine that all those mental programs we've been talking about have been filed away in filing cabinets in a big storage center in your brain. That's not exactly what it looks like inside your head, of course, but it helps to give you an idea of how it works.

Now imagine that we're standing right now in the middle of your computer control center with its walls covered floor-to-ceiling with those filing cabinets where all your programs live.

Picture yourself walking up to one of those filing cabinets and opening a file drawer. There are sections of files on literally every part of your life you can imagine, everything from your family to your education to your self-esteem to your career, and everything in between. If you were to take a look, what do you suppose you'd find in your own personal files?

In those files you would find your dreams, your hopes, your

failings and your fears. In them you would find your strengths and your hesitations, your goals and your uncertainties, and the most complete picture ever found of who you are today, and who you *could* be tomorrow.

And in those files you would find every one of your beliefs—and the script that is even *now* being written for the future that is yet in front of you.

And every thought you think, and every action you take, is *voted on* by every single program file in your brain that could have anything at all to do with what you will do or think next. To show you how this voting process works, let's look at a real-life example.

NO DIAMOND FOR DAVE

A man I knew, named Dave, told me of an incident that happened to him that literally changed his life in a few seconds. I met Dave at a seminar I gave in his city, and during the informal session afterwards, when I was talking with a group of network marketers, he joined in the discussion. "I used to be in network marketing," he said.

Dave went on to tell me he had been successfully working the plan, and his new business was starting to take off. His family was beginning to believe he could actually do something with this, and he and his wife had even had the first of the "what-if" discussions about the day when he could walk away from his insurance job for good.

Then came the morning when Dave was scheduled to show the plan at a breakfast meeting with George, one of his colleagues at work. Dave knew that another network marketer was also actively trying to recruit George, and he could tell that his friend was at a point in life to make a change. The time was exactly right for George to hear what Dave had to say.

He was scheduled to meet George and his wife Betty for breakfast at 7:30 on Saturday morning, so Friday night Dave carefully set his alarm for 5:30. He wanted to be up early enough not only to arrive on time at the meeting, but also to go over the points of his presentation one more time.

At 5:30 on Saturday morning, the alarm went off as scheduled. Half-awake, Dave rolled over and reached his arm out toward the alarm clock on his nightstand. His hand hovered over the two buttons on the clock: the button on the left that would start the radio and begin his day on time, and the one on the right that said "snooze."

WATCH WHAT'S REALLY HAPPENING

At that moment, "freeze-frame" Dave! Stop him right there with his hand in midair, poised to turn off the clock and derail his success, or turn on the radio and launch him into his future.

Now, rush upstairs into Dave's computer control center and watch what's really happening at that precise moment. In that instant, Dave's computer filing cabinets begin flying open at lightning speed! In that same moment, every program in Dave's entire program storage center that has *anything at all* to do with what he will do next, will *vote*. In that instant, all of those programs fly out—and each one votes—with the *stronger* programs always outvoting the *weaker* programs.

Dave's programs on personal motivation, procrastination and getting things done; how well he has done in the past; the programs that tell him whether he believes he's really up to his new success, and whether he deserves it in the first place; the programs that create his security and insecurity; his programs about stability, work, and his responsibility to earn a steady income; the programs that tell him how good he is at setting goals and reaching them; programs from long ago and programs from his recent past; every program about the responses he's received in the past when he showed the plan; his programs of acceptance and rejection; all of his programs of *self-esteem*—who he really is, and everything he believes about himself—in that same moment, all of those programs—and thousands more just like them—*vote!*

And *in that same instant* the vote is tallied up, and the results type themselves across the giant computer screen in Dave's computer control center.

The words about to be written on that screen will determine what Dave will do next. Every program has voted, chemically and electrically, biologically, *neurologically* in his brain—all in a single *instant* of time!

At that moment, on the computer control screen in Dave's internal control center, the words appear:

"OKAY TO SLEEP IN."

Now take Dave out of freeze-frame. In less than the space of a single heartbeat, the decision that will change Dave's future—and his family's future—has been made. Dave's hand reaches for the snooze button, *and he goes back to sleep.*

It's clear to anyone that Dave just made a bad choice. It would prove to hurt him. He missed the meeting with George and Betty, of course, and although George was nice about it when Dave saw him at work on Monday, he could tell the opportunity was lost.

Not long after that, someone else sponsored George and Betty—and by the time I met Dave, he told me that George had left their insurance firm and was now applying his considerable talent and energy full-time toward making his sponsor and himself into Diamonds. And Dave could have been the one to sponsor George. He had gotten *so close.* Success had been nearer to Dave than he could have imagined.

Instead, within a few weeks of that lost opportunity, Dave dropped out of network marketing entirely. There were other contributing factors, of course; sleeping in was just the first step. And although Dave did have the responsibility to make the right decision, *something else was going on* at that critical moment.

WHAT *REALLY* MADE DAVE'S CHOICE?

The truth is that *Dave did not really make a conscious choice at all!* At the time the decision to turn off the alarm was being made, *Dave wasn't even awake!* He didn't stop and think about it, nor was he aware that a vote was being taken. He never made a conscious decision himself. He didn't have to. *Dave's internal programs made the decision for him.*

While he was half-awake, Dave's programs voted, decided, and made him take the wrong action. It was *those* programs that wanted Dave to give up. His old programs wanted Dave to quit trying, to go back to being his *"normal"* self, to fit in and follow the old rules of what life is *supposed* to be like.

It had nothing to do with what Dave *wanted*—it was what his programs were designed to get him to do. No matter how badly he wanted—and needed—to succeed at this one, Dave was *programmed* to fail.

WHAT IF DAVE HAD DIFFERENT PROGRAMS?

What if Dave had different programs—better programs of strong positive self-esteem, programs that made him proud to be in Amway and proud to say so, programs that saw him as deserving of his newfound success, programs of strong self-motivation, and programs of confidence that told him he had everything it would take to sustain his new course of action long enough to build the life he and his family dreamed of?

With *those* kinds of programs, the outcome of Dave's vote would have been completely different. Instead of despair, there would still be a Diamond in his future.

What if someone had been able to help Dave change his old programs? What if he could have gotten past them, traded them in for new programs that would help him create the life he really wanted?

Now put yourself in Dave's place, and think about the action *your* programs might have caused you to take in the same situation. Which button would you have reached for?

Which button do you reach for right now, in every small

decision, every moment of your life? That's a very important question, because it works exactly the same way for us as it did for Dave: *our* programs do most of our voting for us.

Our programs direct and control our lives, in every single action we take—or *fail* to take. And unless we do something to *change* those old programs, we will continue to fail. *The old programs will continue to vote against us.*

WHAT DOES THIS MEAN TO *YOU*, *RIGHT NOW?*

Does this recent research into the human computer brain have any bearing on your life and on your business, right now . . . today?

Yes, it does—more than you might ever have imagined. Those dedicated scientists have unlocked the key to why some people make it, and why the rest of them don't.

The message is clear: *Your attitudes, your beliefs, your fears, your dreams, your choices, your actions, and your ultimate success are tied directly to the programs that are stored somewhere in the filing cabinets in your brain.*

It doesn't make any difference whether we believe that or not. It doesn't make any difference if we accept it or reject it. It is simply medical, biological fact. Programs are real. And nothing we will ever do to try to ignore it, or forget it, will ever change that fact.

It makes sense, then, that if you have programs recorded in your brain right now—and if those programs are getting in your way—then if you could change the programs, you would change the results. In short, you would probably change your entire future.

Imagine what knowing that (and doing something about it) could do for your future as an Amway Distributor: Change the old program pathways in the brain, and you will change the path in front of you.

Imagine what you could do if every single program you had was exactly the *right* program—if every mental direction you gave yourself from now on was designed to build you up, show you what you *can* do, instead of what you *cannot,* and move you forward in life with every step you take! Success would be a lot easier to reach. You would almost certainly reach the level you aim for in the organization, and it would probably take you a lot less time to get there.

Getting rid of some of those old programs could literally change the road to becoming a Diamond, as an example— make it *easier,* more *direct,* more *accessible.* Imagine having the goals you have today, without having to worry about your old programs getting in the way.

If you have one friend who is doing better than another friend, look at each of their programs and ask yourself why one of them is doing better than the other. Almost as soon as you ask the question, you will have the answer.

THE INCREDIBLE DIFFERENCE
YOUR PROGRAMS CAN MAKE

Think of someone you know who is "successful." Not just financially, but in other ways. Think of a person who is doing well overall—achieving, and is clearly destined for even greater things to come. After you have decided on the person you have chosen as a great picture of "success," get a clear picture of that person in your mind. And once you have the name, get a picture of that person talking, taking action, being in control of his or her life.

Then ask yourself the question: *What kind of programs does that person have?*

Now think of someone you know whose life is the opposite of happy and successful—someone who is doing poorly. Not necessarily health-wise or physically, but one who is doing poorly in spirit. Someone who is not succeeding, not happy, and who does not appear to be in control of his life.

What are this person's goals? How is his self-esteem? How does he talk to others? How is his confidence? When he talks, what does he sound like? What kind of words and phrases does he use to express himself? How does he think? How does that person sit; stand; walk? What is the look in that person's eyes?

What kind of programs does that person have?

The first thing that becomes obvious is that there is a remarkable, life-directing difference between these two people. And it is clear that the difference is not just some accident of nature. It is stronger than that. And it is simpler. It is a difference in their programs.

I asked you to look at these two people for a reason. (You could conceivably look at *everyone* you know, and begin to rate each of them on your own personal "programming chart"—though I wouldn't necessarily recommend it!)

All of the people you know end up thinking, believing, making their choices, walking, seeing, and even looking like they do because of the programs they carry with them. It is also true that you, too, and everything you think and do, are a living, breathing picture of the programs that are within you.

TURNING DREAMS INTO DIAMONDS

Pause for a moment and answer this question for yourself: Are you satisfied with the programs you have right now? Do you have any programs you would like to get rid of? Or, if you could, do you have any programs you would like to change?

We have learned that virtually *everything* you think and do to reach your goals, is affected, influenced, or controlled by the programs you carry with you right now. What you do today, tomorrow, and every day from now on, to reach your goals as an Amway Distributor, will be determined by those same programs.

But we have also learned there is a way to get *past* the old programs that have been working against us—and that the brain is designed to *help* us do it. And finally, we have learned *how*.

Let's take a look at what the researchers learned about turning those *old* programs into *new* programs—and turning *dreams* into *diamonds*.

*"Many people use Self-Talk
to make exceptional changes
in the quality of their lives.*

These are the people to watch.

*These are the people
who find real, lasting success
because they have decided
to change their programs
for good."*

Chapter Seven
A Major Breakthrough In Reprogramming

I magine a dedicated team of neuroscientists doing exhaustive research into brain chemistry—*and ending up with a major solution that could help Amway double in size in the next few years.* When they were doing their research, I don't imagine those researchers knew just *how much* they were helping change the world!

A WAY TO GET PAST THE OLD PROGRAMS

We've learned that our programs control a lot more of our lives than we could ever have imagined, and that it is important to change our old programs for the better. But until recently, we didn't know we *could* change our old programs;

and what is most important, we didn't know *how.*

But while they were studying the causes and treatment for Alzheimer's disease, the neuroscientists stumbled upon a discovery that makes all the difference in the world when it comes to getting past the old programs. They found *hope.*

What the researchers discovered not only confirmed that our programs are physical pathways in the brain; they proved we could do something about it. They learned that if a person could somehow *stop using* an old program long enough, the old program would actually break down chemically—*all by itself!* And the change is *physical* in the brain, measurable with sophisticated medical imaging computers.

CHANGING PATHWAYS IN THE BRAIN

We've all heard the expression, "It takes 21 days to change a habit." It's no coincidence those same researchers found out it takes *exactly* the same time—about three weeks—to begin to break down the chemical pathways, which are actually old programs in the brain! What we know as *habits* are the same thing as *programs*, to our mental computers.

But how do we *stop* using an old program long enough to break it down? If you took the disk out of the computer at home or at the office, it would simply stop; it would be unable to function at all. If you wanted that computer to work, without using any of the old programs, you would have to *replace* the old programs with something else—and the brain works the same way.

If we want to get off the old programs, we first have to

replace them with something else. And that's where Self-Talk comes in.

THE BREAKTHROUGH CALLED SELF-TALK

What we call "Self-Talk" is a major breakthrough, a way of replacing old mental programs in the brain with new, positive programs. A variety of Self-Talk techniques are currently being used in schools, hospitals, churches, weight clinics, businesses, and by thousands of salespeople and network marketers across the country. Self-Talk is helping everyone from schoolchildren to medical professionals tackle such issues as self-esteem, counseling, relationships, and personal and professional success.

Hundreds of thousands of people are now using popular Self-Talk methods to make exceptional changes in the quality of their lives—and one of the first groups to recognize the merits of Self-Talk was the group of network marketers made up of Amway members across the nation.

These are the people to watch. These are the people who find real, lasting success, because they have decided to change their programs for good. The results are clear: *Self-Talk works in people's lives, because Self-Talk changes programs.*

In order for you to put Self-Talk techniques into practice in your *own* life, and begin the process of "trading in" your old programs for new ones that work in your favor instead of against you, it will help to begin by finding out what some of your *present* programs look like.

MONITORING YOUR SELF-TALK:
THE FIRST STEP OF CHANGE

This first step is called "Monitoring," and it means just that. Here's how it works:

❑ *For the next several days, listen consciously to everything you say out loud.*

Listen to *every* word that comes out of your mouth. Don't try to change any of what you say or make it better; just listen to it. If you had someone follow you around with a tape recorder, what do you suppose the transcript of three of your average speaking days would sound like?

❑ *Listen for the Self-Talk statements you make about yourself.*

Pay special attention to any comments you make about yourself, comments that describe you or your feelings. From even a casual glance at a few of your monitored statements, it would be easy to see that most of the comments are made without you really thinking about them at all.

That's true of all of us. And the unconscious Self-Talk we use every day is only the "tip of the iceberg." It is a glimpse into the tens of thousands of much larger programs that live and operate deep in all of us.

Fortunately, you don't have to know what all of your programs are in order to change them. But monitoring what you are saying—and thinking—now, will begin to tell you what some of your programs sound like now.

❐ *Monitor the Self-Talk of others around you.*

While you're listening to your own Self-Talk, also pay close attention to the Self-Talk of people around you. There is no better way to recognize the power of a person's Self-Talk than to listen to other people, and then measure *their* Self-Talk, good or bad, against the lives they are leading—or how happy and "successful" they are.

While you are observing this, don't feel obligated to mention people's Self-Talk to them; just be a good observer. You should find it fascinating enough getting to know the programs that drive the people around you, while you're getting to know your own.

MONITOR AND WRITE DOWN YOUR SELF-TALK FOR THE NEXT THREE DAYS

One of the most important steps you can take to discover what your current programs look like, is to *write down* what you hear yourself saying.

For the next three days, I recommend that you carry a pocket notebook with you. (The notes section of your Franklin Planner works well for this.) Keep your notebook handy, and jot down the Self-Talk statements you hear yourself saying as you go about your normal activities.

This Self-Talk monitor log will help you to consciously *listen* to *everything* you say for the next three days. Make a list, even if it only includes a few samples of your everyday Self-Talk.

Your Self-Talk monitor log may have only as many as a dozen or two entries. That's not many when you consider you may make hundreds of Self-Talk statements in two or three days. But even a short list will begin to give you the idea.

☐ *Ask your family or your friends to help you with your list.*

Ask the people close to you to help you with this. They will often hear you say things that you aren't aware of saying yourself. If you're planning on tackling your new Self-Talk project privately, you can skip this one. Otherwise, consider asking for outside input.

☐ *Read your list over carefully and ask yourself what it tells you.*

After three days of keeping your monitor log, read it over several times to yourself. The results of your list should not be difficult for you to analyze for yourself. The following questions will help:

1. What does your list of your own Self-Talk statements tell you?

2. Is your Self-Talk usually self-enhancing or self-effacing? That is, does most of your Self-Talk build you up, put you down, or let you stay even?

3. Is it the kind of Self-Talk that you would like to actively program into your own computer? Would you type those same statements as lifelong directives into your own internal computer keyboard?

4. What are the strongest programs that showed up on your list?

5. What were your programs about network marketing in general, and about Amway in particular?

6. Did you have any programs that came up more than once?

7. Did you find any programs you'd like to change?

We're not looking for an in-depth analysis here—nor do we need one. This is a starter exercise; it's designed to quickly boost your awareness of your own Self-Talk programs and the programs of the people around you.

This first technique is not designed to create long-term changes in your programs. It is, however, an important first step in the right direction—and the next step is even more important.

THE NEXT STEP: *EDITING* YOUR SELF-TALK

This next technique will help you start to turn your Self-Talk around. It sounds simple, but doing it can begin to make a major difference in the programs that control your direction, right now.

❒ *Begin immediately EDITING your own Self-Talk when you're talking.*

Each time you find yourself about to say something the old way, change the statement to reflect the new programs you wish to create. You don't have to be an expert at translating Self-Talk to begin editing what you say, even as you say it. With a little practice you'll find that not only does it get easier, but in a short time you'll also find yourself beginning to edit your own Self-Talk automatically, and very naturally.

For example, if your old Self-Talk statement is *"I don't even want to face going to work today. I wish I could just go back to sleep,"* at the moment you say it or even start to think it, change it to new Self-Talk that sounds like this:

"I'm awake, alive, full of energy and full of life—and today is a great day to prove it!"

When you do this, not only do you get a much healthier program at that moment, but you also give a strong message to your subconscious mind. You're literally saying to yourself, *"This is the way I choose to be from here on out; this is the kind of program I want you to help me create."*

If that sounds like *you,* giving directions to *you,* it *is.* Strange as it may sound to you at first, that kind of strong, clear, no-nonsense message to your own internal self is one of the most important steps you can take to begin changing the programs that have gotten in your way.

Editing your own Self-Talk as you speak is easy to do. It literally takes no time. And once you get into the practice of editing your own Self-Talk, it becomes a habit in itself, and you end up creating programs that reinforce the positive habit—so the more you do it, the more you do it.

ANOTHER IMPORTANT BENEFIT

Editing your own Self-Talk *while* you're talking or thinking is an important step in beginning to change the old programs. But editing has another, more immediate benefit as well. The effect of speaking it, declaring it, hearing it, and taking action on your new self-directions right now, ends up changing choices that would otherwise have been made for you unconsciously—by your old programs.

When you practice editing your Self-Talk, you will find yourself making better choices almost immediately. You will already begin to exercise more control.

For more examples of how your new Self-Talk should sound, refer to the scripts in Chapters Eight, Thirteen, and Sixteen. The more you read the scripts, or listen to them on tape, the better idea you'll have of how to turn your own words around before they have a chance to send your day off-course.

WHAT IF IT SOUNDS TOO PERFECT?

The problem with changing old negative Self-Talk to the new, more "positive" Self-Talk, is that at first the new version could seem too . . . *perfect*—like you're trying to get yourself to talk or think in a way that *no one* could live up to. When you first hear the statements, you could easily shake your head in disbelief, as though you're kidding yourself.

Imagine reading the following Self-Talk statements to

yourself, or hearing them on a tape every morning:

"I do everything I need to do to make my business work—today especially!"

"Today is a great day to show the plan, and that's what I plan to do today."

"I'm proud to be in Amway—and it shows!"

Many of your old programs, exactly the kind of programs you'd like to get rid of, will get you to look at a sentence of the new kind of Self-Talk and almost make fun of its absurdity. *"You're kidding yourself,"* the old programs tell you. *"Nobody talks that way—especially not you."*

But that is immediate proof that the new Self-Talk ought to be taken *very* seriously. After all, if your own negative programs of the past immediately try to get you to *disbelieve* the new Self-Talk, what does that tell you? It says that given a chance, the old programs would like to stop you—*right now*, before you ever let the new, *positive* programs try to make their way into your life.

The more unusual, the more different and *alive* your new Self-Talk sounds, the more *seriously* you should take it.

WHEN YOU CHANGE WHAT YOU SAY, YOU CHANGE THE WHOLE DAY

What if someone were to tell you that you could get in

control of your day in just ten seconds? Would you believe it?

It's entirely true that the process of editing your Self-Talk "on the fly" takes about ten seconds to do. But the effects of that change can turn around your entire day—and often, the day of everyone around you. As it turns out, positive Self-Talk is contagious!

❐ *Use turning your Self-Talk around as a direct motivational tool to help you control your attitude each day.*

One of the most important reasons for learning this technique is that it ends up being highly motivational—you end up being a better *self*-motivator. And every time you turn your Self-Talk around, you get better at it.

Another advantage to this technique is that you get instant results. You get positive attention from other people. You *feel* better every time you make a new Self-Talk statement clearly and with conviction.

That's because when you create positive enthusiasm by the way you speak to yourself and to others, you also change the chemicals in your brain that make you feel better. And that's not only good for your state of mind—it's also good for your success rate.

Turn your old Self-Talk around. Change it. Reword it, transform it, and watch the pictures it begins to create—even *thinking* about it being *true* in your life.

Using this Self-Talk editing technique seldom takes longer than a few seconds. Like a lot of other people who have tried it, you'll soon recognize that getting the job done as a successful distributor is not the major battle it could seem to be. It is a lot of *little* moments, the smallest skirmishes of will and self-control. If you want to succeed, you will.

Monitoring your Self-Talk should greatly increase your awareness of the programs you have, and *editing* can help you begin to change the programs you want to get rid of. If you want to build success for yourself in Amway, and in the rest of your life, begin now to change your programs every chance you get—*as many times a day as it takes* to be successful.

In the next chapter, we'll look at specific examples of Self-Talk that will help you build your new programs—and your business—as an Amway Distributor.

*"If you get the right programs
working for you,
you have a good chance
of staying motivated
and staying with it.*

*After all,
success is a great motivator!"*

Chapter Eight

Getting Motivated And
Staying Motivated

I f you have been with Amway for any time at all, you have probably experienced those *amazing* Amway weekends. It is at those events that you get remotivated, revitalized, recommitted, reminded, and renewed.

But eventually, and all too soon, the weekend draws to a close, and it's time to go back to the world of your everyday life.

What happens when that incredibly worthwhile weekend is over, the motivation and the inspiring words are gone, and you're back home again, and on your own? How long does your own, *internal* motivation last? Two weeks? Two days? A few hours?

It really wasn't *your* motivation at all. It was motivation on loan from someone else, people who had more than enough to give away, and were caring enough to share their motivation with you for a time.

And then you go back to your life, and your work, and your routine, and back to your *old programs*.

That isn't to say those incredible weekends aren't some of the best experiences you could ever take part in. Those weekends are *essential* if you really want to succeed in the Amway business. And what I'm going to share with you now are some tools to help you build new programs to make that motivation *last*—and to create nonstop motivation for yourself, not just now and then, but every day.

MAKING *EVERY* DAY AN AMWAY DAY

Motivation is a state of mind. And if that motivation is the kind that comes to you from someone else, then it is also a *temporary* state of mind. It feels great while it lasts, but it will eventually go away.

That's because that great, elated feeling you feel is induced by natural *chemical changes in the brain* that take place only while you're being motivated. Later, those chemical changes revert back to their normal state, and the feeling of elation is gone.

It is a natural, automatic chemical process. And that is why external, outside, *momentary* motivation never lasts. It cannot.

Knowing that, it has always been my goal to teach people how to create that same motivation *within themselves*. Attend every meeting, rally, event, and function you can. Don't miss a single opportunity to learn more; associate with the right kind of people—and get motivated.

But at the same time, if you know how to be your own best motivator, you never have to worry about the motivator going home—you *are* the motivator! And you get to recreate that excitement and enthusiasm for any reason, at any time at all.

Imagine being able to attend your next exciting weekend Amway function, learning new ideas, recommitting to your goals, getting pumped up with unstoppable enthusiasm and determination—and then taking it all *with* you when you leave—and *staying* motivated *after* you get home!

The people who learn how to create *self*-motivation are among the most successful people you will ever meet:

- They tackle problems more positively. They are able to get past obstacles faster and more easily.

- They have more energy, they get more things done, so they have more time.

- They are better at prospecting and showing the plan, because their own positive motivation is inspiring to the people who are seeing the plan.

- They attract other positive, like-minded people, so they are surrounded with the kind of people who can help them reach even higher levels of success.

- Because they are constantly reaching their goals, their self-esteem is healthy and strong.

And they excel in all of this, because they have learned *self*-motivation.

SPECIAL SELF-TALK
FOR AMWAY DISTRIBUTORS

Over the years, I have written, published, and recorded several hundred in-depth Self-Talk scripts. Those scripts have included specialized Self-Talk for children, for parents, for motivation, self-esteem, spiritual strength, and a host of other important Self-Talk programs that people wanted to incorporate into their lives. In time, many of those Self-Talk programs—those internal messages—became a positive, working part of many people's successes.

But until recently, I had never written, or recorded, Self-Talk scripts that I had developed specifically for Amway Distributors.

But now, because you are a member of that organization (or are soon going to be), and because I believe strongly in what you are doing, here for the first time is a special series of Self-Talk "Amway" scripts, just for you.

This is Self-Talk—in its clearest, most direct form. It is like a list of choices—*from* you, and *to* you, expecting you to live up to your best, and at the same time, showing you exactly what you need to do next.

As you read through these scripts, I should caution you. What you read in the scripts themselves will sound disarmingly simple. The words, themselves, won't look like they could change your life.

But listen to the new "programs," and watch the new pictures in your mind, that the words create. And then imagine making these same, new Self-Talk programs a part of your life for the next weeks, or months, or years.

For now, while you read the words, just imagine these

programs becoming part of who you are, and what you do, every future day of your Amway career.

SELF-TALK FOR STAYING MOTIVATED

What kind of Self-Talk could help you through those days when nothing seems to work? What about those moments, or those days, when you're not quite "there" yet—when things don't always work out right, or when too many people in a row tell you no (or they're going to *think* about it)?

I know that if I were there with you, in person, on those days, I would probably start by giving you a very direct heart-to-heart talk about how good you *really* are, what you *can* do, and how successful you're going to be. I would convince you of the *truth* about yourself.

But if I can't be there in person, this first script of Self-Talk can help. It is called *"Getting Motivated and* Staying *Motivated,"* and it is written for you, for those times when you want to be on top of the world—but it feels like the world is on top of you.

SPECIAL AMWAY DISTRIBUTOR
SELF-TALK SCRIPT #1:

"GETTING MOTIVATED AND STAYING *MOTIVATED"*

I am motivated! I choose to be IN MOTION, right now!

I have goals. I have dreams. I have plans. I have a job

to do. And nothing is going to stop me from reaching my goal, living my dream, following my plan, and getting my job done!

I do everything I need to do, when I need to do it. I get things done. Today especially!

I feel good. My thinking is clear and sharp. I have a precise picture of what I have to do, and I am determined to take action, get the job done, and enjoy the rewards I create.

I put myself into motion. I have enthusiasm. I feel great! My attitude is tops. My courage is contagious. Everyone around me knows that "today is definitely my day."

I motivate myself, and I motivate others. I believe in myself, and I believe in the people I add to my Amway team.

This is my moment! Today is my day. I take action, and I get things done!

I really enjoy being excited by the work I'm doing with Amway. I especially like the positive energy it creates in my life.

I keep myself motivated by motivating others. The more energy I help them create, the more motivation I create for myself!

An accurate description of me would include the words: energetic, positive, excited to be alive, filled with enthusiasm, determined to succeed, happy, and very motivated!

My attitude is really great. I feel good about myself; I like working the plan; I really enjoy being successful, and my motivation has never been better!

I start each day by making sure I'm motivated. I review my checklist, I get a clear picture of my dream, and I go for it!

I choose to feel great, on top of the world, and going for it!

Right now, at this moment, I make the choice to believe in myself, and enjoy every moment of creating my success!

I am MOTIVATED!

Imagine listening to that one Self-Talk script each morning when you wake up—or even reading through it as you start your day!

When you are proud of who you are, and what you're doing, your enthusiasm shows. Imagine having that kind of belief in Amway the next time you meet someone new, or the next time you make a presentation. If you want other people to believe, you have to be *alive* with that same belief yourself! When you make that kind of Self-Talk a permanent part of who you are, you are literally *creating* that faith within you.

You'll notice that all correctly scripted Self-Talk is *always* stated in the *present* tense. It is Self-Talk that says to your own internal computer, "This is how I *choose* to be . . . now let's get to work on it." So you are giving yourself a *completed* picture of how you choose to be in the future.

Self-Talk, when you use it in the right way, is much more than words. It becomes a part of who you are. With this next Amway Self-Talk script, as an example, you can literally give yourself the kind of programs that change how you look at making presentations.

SELF-TALK FOR SHOWING THE PLAN

Do you ever hesitate? Are you always as effective as you'd like to be? Do your faith and enthusiasm come through as strongly as they should? Do you look forward with excited anticipation to showing the plan every chance you get?

Start making this next script of Self-Talk programs a part of your own internal programming, and watch what begins to happen with every presentation you make.

SPECIAL AMWAY DISTRIBUTOR SELF-TALK SCRIPT #2:

"SHOWING THE PLAN"

I really like presenting the Amway opportunity—every chance I get. I believe in Amway, and I believe in this plan.

I am helping people change their lives. I am showing them a better way. I am opening the door to their unlimited futures.

I care about the people I am talking to, and it shows.

I like being in front of people. I express myself well. And people like what I have to say.

I practice getting better with every presentation I make. Every time I show the plan, is a chance for me to improve.

I have confidence in myself. I have faith in my dreams. I believe in the incredible opportunity I am sharing. And it shows in every word I say.

I greet every Amway presentation I make, with the enthusiasm of my belief, the appreciation for the opportunity to share, and the certainty of my success.

I like people. I see everyone I meet as someone whose life will be better because I was there.

I am thankful for the chance to help people in a way that is good, true, and valuable. The plan I show is filled with positive opportunity for their lives.

Each time I show the plan, I am giving people a way to add even more value and meaning to their lives.

I never put off showing the plan. I set my goal, follow the steps, schedule the meeting, and create my success.

Showing the plan, and sharing the dream, are a way of life for me.

Every morning when I awake, I think of the people whose lives I will help this day. Because of Amway, and because I show the plan, I have a lot to be thankful for.

I am excited with my life! I can't wait to show the plan again. I show the plan . . . and I succeed!

Just making those powerful programs a part of your life could make a real difference in how well you show the plan—and how often! If you follow the plan yourself, you're going to succeed. And if you get the *right programs* working for you, you have a good chance of staying motivated and staying with it—and working the plan. When you do that, your motivation goes up. After all, *success* is a *great* motivator.

SELF-TALK FOR TAKING ACTION NOW

You should read or listen to this next script anytime you want to feel good about yourself and the actions you're taking to move yourself forward in your life. Even while you read it, imagine your internal coach talking to you, boosting your courage, building your enthusiasm, pushing, encouraging, motivating you to put yourself into motion.

Being "in motion," with the right plan, is what true motivation is all about. Because you're working with Amway, you already have the right plan. Now let's see if we can add more of the incredible power of forward motion—and watch what happens to that plan. If you practice the following Self-Talk, and actively work to get your programs just right, your day—and your *results*—are about to change.

SPECIAL AMWAY DISTRIBUTOR
SELF-TALK SCRIPT #3:

"I TAKE ACTION, NOW!"

I take action NOW!

I choose to win with Amway. So I set goals, I manage my time, and I get things done.

I have a clear picture of what I want to accomplish. I set priorities, I plan my day, and I follow my plan.

I visualize my success every day. Right now, at this moment, I see myself doing those things that improve my business and create my success.

I get things done, on time, and in the right way.

I never let negative attitudes of any kind, stand in my way. I am positive, enthusiastic, and I actively work the plan.

I see problems as nothing more than the stepping stones to my success.

When I see a problem, I study it, I determine the solution, I see a clear picture of my goal, and I put myself into action!

I know that I can achieve any goal I set for myself. I am strong, determined, motivated, and certain of my success.

I always get the help I need, to get the job done right.

99

I attend every Amway function and meeting that is available to me! I use the tools, the ideas, and the support I'm offered—and I insure my success!

I improve myself in some way, every day of my life. I read, I listen, I learn, and I win!

I associate with other people who know how to get things done. I spend my time with positive, motivated, successful people—just like me!

Every day, I create the success habit of taking action. I choose to win . . . so I take action—NOW!

I know what to do, and I know how to do it. Today is the day I get things done!

I take personal and positive responsibility for every action I take today. I choose to make today count!

I am a winner with Amway. I choose to make today an AMWAY day—and I TAKE ACTION, NOW!

Even just reading those words, begins to create actual *chemical* changes in the brain. You can almost *feel* it happening. Imagine *living* those words—*day after day.* It makes you literally get up and go for it!

Now imagine making those same new programs *permanent.* Having the new Self-Talk programs for life is exactly like learning a new language. But this time, it's a language that can build a business, and change your life.

"Any tool you try to use
will always stop working
if it is too difficult.

If it isn't simple,
it will not work."

Chapter Nine
Listening To Self-Talk

This next technique is important if you're interested in long-term change—if you want to do something now that will help you *now,* but also help you change your old programs *permanently.* This technique is also one of the best we have found to greatly improve motivation, attitudes, and actions!

CHANGING YOUR PROGRAMS

As we mentioned, the medical researchers have learned that in order to change or get rid of old programs—the old neuron pathways in the brain—you have to *replace* them with something else. When you override an old program *often enough* with the right new program, the old program literally breaks down, physically and chemically, in your brain, so the old program loses its control. That's when the new program can take over.

Your old programs are something like *highways* in the brain. When you stop using the old programs long enough, it is like a highway that hasn't been driven on in a long time, one that becomes filled with cracks and weeds, and breaks apart—because it is no longer being *maintained.*

So imagine getting off the old highways—the old program pathways—for good. In time, *the neuron pathways begin to break down.* The secret is that you have to create *new* highways, *new programs* to take the place of the old.

That's exactly what listening to Self-Talk does. Self-Talk, with *repeated use,* creates brand new neuron pathways—program highways—in the brain. And *this* time, your programs are the *right* programs.

A PRACTICAL SOLUTION THAT CAN HELP

People have been using the technique of listening to cassette tapes to learn Self-Talk for a long time. After more than a decade of Self-Talk tape listening, it's hard for some of us to remember a time when this tool was not around.

This Self-Talk technique started almost by accident, but it has played a significant role in my life now for more than fifteen years. Although these days Self-Talk tapes are used for every conceivable area of self-help, I first used the technique in the area of weight-loss, because I had lived with a difficult weight problem for many years. I would lose weight, but I would gain it back again. I tried everything, and nothing worked.

At that time, Self-Talk was still in its infancy. I was doing the original pioneering work in Self-Talk several years before writing my first book on the subject, and I was impressed with what I was discovering even then.

In those days, Self-Talk was being used by only three groups of people—Olympic athletes, commercial airline pilots, and NASA astronauts. I decided to try Self-Talk for weight-loss; I figured if Self-Talk would work to help people lose weight, it was strong enough to help them do anything *else* they wanted to do, too.

No one at that time had ever suggested that one day people would be using Self-Talk to improve their marriages or earn more income or build self-esteem, or any of the many areas that Self-Talk is being used for today. We didn't know at that time that one day, thousands of Amway distributors everywhere would be using Self-Talk tapes to help them change their mental programs and improve every area of their business and personal lives.

But the more I studied the subject of Self-Talk and the growing field of motivational psychology, the more it became clear to me that Self-Talk was destined to do far more than help us send astronauts to the moon or win gold medals at the Olympics.

"What about the rest of us?" I wondered. "If we took the time to learn how to use it properly, what could Self-Talk do for *us*?"

I had already spent several years studying the natural programming process of Self-Talk, and working on how the special "scripting" of Self-Talk had to be worded.

I knew that if the new Self-Talk programs were clear

enough, and strong enough, and repeated just so, tied to a goal, and stayed with for a long enough period of time, the new programs would stick: the Self-Talk would get programmed in and it would stay there.

I also knew that if a new program, worded carelessly or in the wrong way, were introduced as Self-Talk, that new—*incorrect*—program would *also* stick.

PUTTING SELF-TALK INTO PRACTICE

So I got an idea.

Although it turned out not to be so, I thought it was a very bright idea at the time. I decided to write out the right kind of Self-Talk on stacks of 3X5 cards, and tape them in neat rows, around and around my mirror where I shaved each morning, leaving a small space in the mirror big enough for me to see to shave. My dressing mirror was the large two-sink kind, and I covered that mirror with *dozens and dozens* of Self-Talk cards.

After years of study, I knew how to write the new Self-Talk phrases exactly right, and I knew that facing me on the mirror each morning would be precisely the programs I would need to achieve my goal.

And so I began. I set my goal to lose fifty pounds, at about two or three pounds a week, while I followed my other goal: to faithfully read through all of my new Self-Talk cards each morning and each night for the next five or six months.

The first morning I got up, faced my mirror, and while I was shaving, I began my reading of the fabulous new Self-Talk programs out loud, stating and restating each carefully-crafted phrase in just the right way. I pictured each thought in my mind as I spoke the words. I projected the phrases with poetic emphasis and filled each thought with determination and feeling.

And sure enough, something happened; *I got late for work.* But I had set a goal, so the next morning I got up and tried it again. I followed my plan, paced carefully again through each specially written phrase of the Self-Talk, repeated it again and again, in just the right way—and got late for work again!

IF IT'S TOO DIFFICULT, IT WON'T WORK

I tried to stay with that first Self-Talk goal. But then, as you might guess, my old programs put a stop to it. It was too difficult, too time-consuming, *too out of the ordinary* for it to work for long.

Anything that is too hard to do simply gives our old programs a chance to come back in and *stop* us. That's one of the reasons why anything we do to change our programs long-term, has to be *easy* enough that the old programs won't stop us even before we get started.

Any tool you try to use to change programs will always stop working if it's too difficult. If it isn't *simple*, it will not work.

That's why my "bright idea" didn't work.

I was disappointed, of course, but I was determined not to give up. I was *convinced* there had to be a way to program my Self-Talk without putting myself through a tough morning regimen that was impossible to follow.

I considered having someone else read the Self-Talk to me, like having a personal trainer helping motivate me every morning. But my wife was as busy as I was, and she didn't have the time to stand there reading Self-Talk out loud to me for fifteen or twenty minutes every morning.

Next I tried memorizing the Self-Talk, thinking that once I had committed the words and phrases to memory, I could deliver a morning soliloquy of Self-Talk that would surely sink into my subconscious mind and deliver me from my tribulations forever. But that didn't work any better than the reading ritual; trying to memorize the Self-Talk was even harder.

THERE HAD TO BE AN EASIER WAY

Because of all the difficulties I had, I finally decided there had to be an easier way. If there wasn't, I believed, I might never find the solution I was looking for. And it was in looking for an easier way that I finally came upon the idea of putting Self-Talk on tape.

"I've tried all the hard ways to reach my goal, and none of them worked," I thought. "Maybe what I need, maybe what we *all* need, is an *easy* way out."

My reasoning about the tapes was very straightforward: We already knew Self-Talk worked. It had to, because it worked the same way the brain was designed to get programmed in the first place: by hearing the programs repeated over and over. But the process would have to be so simple that literally anyone could do it.

I further reasoned that the new Self-Talk would have to be learned without having to work at it, naturally, just like we had gotten our earlier programs to begin with.

Although this was years ago, and at the time no one was using cassettes for anything like Self-Talk, it was clear to me that putting the right Self-Talk on tape would be a perfect solution to the problem. And as it turned out, I was right.

I first tried recording the Self-Talk myself, in my own voice, but eventually I took all of the Self-Talk to a professional recording studio and had it recorded in a professional voice—not my own.

I already suspected then, what I learned later to be true. Before I knew better, I had even written about, and tried to teach others, how to record Self-Talk for themselves. In time, we found that process seldom worked. In fact, during the following years, while I continued to work with Self-Talk and teach it to others, we learned an important new rule:

Never, ever, listen to Self-Talk—on tape—in your own voice.

There are two important reasons for this:

- The first is that you grow up listening to outside voices of authority and the opinions of others before your own.

- The second reason is even more important. Every time you listen to Self-Talk in your own voice on a tape, *you are literally opening up the same old program files that you are trying to close up and get rid of!*

When you listen to your own voice, played back to you on tape, you automatically tend to be *critical* of how you sound.

(What does *that* tell you about your old programs?) On tape, you don't sound like you think you *should*.

Instead of hearing the *right* new Self-Talk messages, you begin to focus on the imperfections in your own recorded words. Hearing yourself while you are just talking is different from hearing your *recorded* voice.

What we usually say is, *"That doesn't sound like* me*!"* And it is that "outside" mechanical sound of your own voice on tape that works against you.

●

SETTING A NEW KIND OF GOAL

In my own case, I finally got the professionally recorded tapes and set a day to begin. This time I set a new kind of goal. I simply agreed with myself to play the tapes each day, and listen. Anything beyond that would have to be up to the tapes themselves.

So once again I got up the first morning with the goal to start my day with Self-Talk. But this time, instead of trying to follow a difficult regimen, I put the first tape into a small cassette player on the counter top in my bathroom, and pressed the button marked "Play."

I didn't get late for work that morning—or any of the mornings that followed. I shaved, got ready, and went about my day. I didn't spend any extra time or make my listening a difficult task. I just listened.

I played the new Self-Talk tapes every morning. I listened to them at night, just before I went to sleep, and when I could during the day. I let the tapes play mostly in the background, and after awhile, I even forgot to focus on them or notice them at all. They were just there, playing quietly as I got ready for my day or went about my life.

Meanwhile, the Self-Talk they contained began to become a part of my life. At first it became a part of my *thinking,* and then *the things I said,* and then, almost without my noticing it, *the new Self-Talk became a part of my actions.*

What was taking place, I noticed, was exactly what happens when we are children, learning a new language for the first time. We learned our language first by hearing, without even thinking about it; then by speaking, until, in time, without even trying to learn them, the words we heard became a permanent part of our life.

With my new Self-Talk, I got the results I was after, and then some. During the next ten-and-a-half weeks I lost *fifty-eight* pounds—shaving—and listening to Self-Talk on tapes! In listening to Self-Talk, a whole new world opened up for me. I had changed my programs; *it worked!*

I was impressed with my results, of course. But what *really* impressed me was that during the same ten-and-a-half weeks I was listening to the tapes, my wife was putting on her makeup at the other end of the same mirror each morning. And during the same ten-and-a-half weeks, *she lost twenty-five pounds eavesdropping on my cassettes.* Her old programs got "outweighed" right along with mine!

In my own story, I learned that with the right Self-Talk, used in the right way, I had indeed changed my programs— *permanently.* That was fifteen years ago. I weigh less today than I did then. And I have never been on a diet since.

It all began with my goal to change my programs about my weight—and now, people everywhere are getting the same positive results in every *other* area of their lives as well!

110

LISTENING TO SELF-TALK IS SOMETHING YOU SHOULD TRY FOR YOURSELF

Not everyone will choose to listen to Self-Talk on tapes. Some people never get around to it. Others find it hard to believe that anything will ever get rid of the old programs. I can understand that. I have been a skeptic myself, and I, too, was cautious until I saw the results in my own life.

Then, too, during the past few years the whole idea of listening to self-improvement tapes has become a popular pastime, and we have been given a lot of promises. And so many tapes sounded so much like each other that it seemed if we'd heard one of them, we'd heard them all. How could Self-Talk on tapes be any different?

Yet Self-Talk on tape *is* different. What you hear on a Self-Talk tape is nothing like we are used to hearing on typical motivational tape programs. Self-Talk tapes are, instead, word for word phrases of a *new language*—except the "new" language is actually the new programs of Self-Talk. So what you hear are the precise kinds of programs you *should* have been getting in the first place—like starting over again, but this time getting it right.

If you could, right now, type completely new programs into your own subconscious mind, but this time create the programs that would build your self-esteem and put *you* firmly in control, the Self-Talk on the tapes is exactly what your new programs would sound like. This time, *you* get to choose what gets typed in!

In fact, not only is learning the new Self-Talk just by listening to it a good idea, but it is the *best* of the tools we have found to put Self-Talk into practice—both easily and rapidly. And therein lies the problem.

I WANTED SELF-TALK TO BE AVAILABLE
TO EVERYONE

For a long time it didn't seem *fair* to me that the one solution we knew to be the *best* solution would be listening to Self-Talk on tapes. Tape listening was, at that time, not something that was immediately available to everybody.

So for some time this remarkably *effective* technique of changing our programs by listening to Self-Talk, while it made a great deal of sense, left me in a quandary. I knew I had found the answer I was looking for, but how could I get that answer into the hands of other people, just like me, who needed it most? I wanted the solution to be something that was easily available to *everyone.*

I also wanted to avoid recommending any Self-Talk techniques that cost anything—even if it was only a small amount. I knew that would only give some people an excuse to put off doing anything with the idea—no matter *how* good the idea was.

And I felt great concern about people seeing Self-Talk only as a commercial idea. There were already too many ideas making the rounds that seemed to be more concerned with commercial appeal than results. I had nothing against prosperity—I believed in it. But I had always felt that Self-Talk somehow went beyond all that. To my way of thinking, Self-Talk had the potential to help an awful lot of people—if I could just get it *to* them.

112

GETTING SELF-TALK TO THE PEOPLE
WHO WANT TO USE IT

I finally concluded that I would simply present the solutions I had found to an audio cassette publisher. That way the people who wanted to listen to Self-Talk tapes could do so. If the publisher agreed to produce the tapes, they would at least be available to everyone who needed them. The publisher said yes, and the first professionally recorded Self-Talk Cassettes were finally released to the public.

Now, years later, and nearly a million Self-Talk tape listeners later, I am *still* listening to Self-Talk on tape. I don't have to listen to Self-Talk for weight-loss anymore, of course. My problem with weight went away a long time ago. Now I listen to Self-Talk that will help me achieve *other* goals—like having more time in a day—and getting my books written on time.

SOME IMPORTANT HINTS

1. Your programs are going to be very important to your success. Make sure you get them right.

If you choose to listen to Self-Talk on tape, avoid the effort of trying to record your own tapes, and don't make the mistake of having a friend record them so they will be in another voice. Listening to Self-Talk is easy, but getting the new programs *exactly right* is a serious matter. Homemade versions often work against you instead of for you. Almost no one has the experience needed to program the right Self-Talk. That would be like trying to record your own Spanish-language learning tapes, when you don't speak Spanish yet.

If you listen at all, listen to professionally recorded cassettes. To do anything less would be to stop yourself from achieving the results you deserve. The professionally produced tapes are now easy enough to obtain, and their cost is minor in comparison to what they do for you.

If you do decide that you'd like to use tapes, there are some listening hints that will help you immediately. During the past ten years or more, with so many thousands of Self-Talk tape listeners, we have learned a lot about how to use the tapes. Although the tape publisher supplies a very concise listening guide with the cassettes, the following guidelines will help you get started:

2. Always play the tapes *quietly* in the background, while you are doing something else.

Self-Talk is *not* like subliminal messages which can't actually be heard or picked up by your brain. (Nor is Self-Talk anything like hypnosis, or "New Age"—in fact, it is the *opposite*.) The words you hear on a Self-Talk tape are based on solid medical and neurological research, and you hear every word out loud, so you always know *exactly* what you're typing into your mental computer.

Don't focus or concentrate on the tapes. The Self-Talk should be played just loud enough to be heard, but quietly, while you are going about your normal activities.

Listening to Self-Talk on tape should never take a single extra minute out of your day; in fact, most people find it *adds* time, because it increases your motivation and your effectiveness. Remember, the easier you make it, the better it works.

3. There are three special "groups" of Self-Talk tapes: *"Morning," "Daytime,"* and *"Night-time"* tapes.

Listen to the *Morning* tapes as close to when you wake up as possible. They can literally change your day for you that day. They help by creating new programs, but they also affect your mental "chemistry" that day, too.

Listen to the *Night-time* tapes just before you go to sleep or even while you're going to sleep. Most people sleep better and wake up more relaxed. That isn't the main purpose of the Self-Talk, but it's a nice side benefit.

The *Daytime* tapes can be listened to anytime during the day, but many people have found that driving in the car is an especially good time and place to listen.

4.   Don't stop listening to your Amway tapes just because you start using Self-Talk.

The Self-Talk you get from the tapes should *tie in* with what your Amway tapes tell you, not *compete* with them. Just keep listening to the tapes provided to you by your organization, and add Self-Talk. You'll notice that your other tapes should start to work even *better* for you, as the old negative programs begin to go away.

5.   The primary purpose of listening to Self-Talk on tapes is to *change your programs.*

You may decide to listen to Self-Talk tapes just because they *motivate* you and make you feel better about yourself— even if you're not concerned about changing old programs.

Remember, though, the goal here is to create *permanent change.* I recommend that if you do choose to listen, you follow a very simple but consistent listening plan; it is the *repetition* of your new programs that allows them to eventually outvote your old negative programs, and put *you* back in control. And the more you listen, the better it works.

When you are working on changing your old programs, the special Self-Talk scripts I've provided for you here in this book will help a great deal, whether you choose to read them daily or listen to them on tape. (If you would like to obtain professional cassette recordings of the six Amway scripts in this book, I have included the cassette publisher's name and address in the back of the book for your convenience.)

If you *do* choose to listen, be sure to follow the guidelines I've outlined for you in this chapter, to receive the maximum programming benefit from your tapes.

Self-Talk tapes aren't magic, and they're not designed to create overnight miracles. Nothing that is "real" and lasting does. But if you use the tapes as you are instructed to, they can help you make some very important changes in your success with Amway *and* in the rest of your life.

If you'd like to take permanent control of your own programs, the easiest and most effective way to practice your new Self-Talk is by *listening* to it.

Part III
Going For It

*"If you were to step forward
in time, right now,
and if you were to
sit down and look through
a photograph album of you
in that future . . .*

*What kind of pictures
of your tomorrows
would you see?"*

Chapter Ten
10 Snapshots Of
Network Marketers

Our main objective is to find the programs that work *against* you, and *change* them. Or determine the programs that work *for* you, and create *more* of them, so that you can reach the level of success in Amway that you want to reach.

To do that you have to get a clearer picture of where you might be today. Where have your old programs led you up to now? If you know that, you have a much better idea of what to do next.

The person who puts things off can start changing the programs that caused him to put things off. The person who works hard, but is always running off in unfocused directions, can get a much clearer focus on which one, single direction to follow. The person who doubts his future with Amway, instead of believing—can now *change the programs* that caused the doubt in the first place!

A PHOTOGRAPH OF YOUR FUTURE

If you were to step forward in time, right now, and if you were to sit down and look through a photograph album of you in *your* future, what kind of pictures of your tomorrows would you see?

Would you be spending your time the way you'd like to spend your time in the future?

Would you be helping others, and watching them achieve their goals while you're achieving yours?

Would you be controlling your own destiny—working for yourself, and deciding what you'd like to do, when you want to do it?

Would you have more money in the bank than you would ever need? Would the people you care about be safe, and financially secure?

Would you see yourself waking up and greeting every new day like it was the most important day in your life—and while you're at it, surrounding yourself with people you love?

Would you see yourself being able to add the free time—to work on that special project you've always wanted to take the time to do?

Would you get to know your kids while they still recognize you're one of their parents?

Would you see yourself traveling, going to new places, and enriching your life with new knowledge and experience?

Would you be living the life you would really want to live?

If you could, right now, see yourself in your own future, what would you choose to see?

10 SNAPSHOTS OF NETWORK MARKETERS

To get a picture of where you are right now, let us look at a few snapshots—accurate pictures of the people around you who are involved in network marketing right now. You will probably recognize most of the people we are spotlighting. Some people you know will fit more than one category. And somewhere on this list, in two or three places, you should find some pictures of yourself.

Let's take a look at just 10 simple snapshots—ten pictures of people in network marketing—and let us consider their chances for success, their programs, and what they can do to get where they want to go.

PICTURE #1: "THE STEALTH DISTRIBUTOR"

Basic operating style: *Invisible*

If you met a Stealth Distributor, you probably wouldn't know it. These people are the *"I'm a member but I really won't admit it,"* networkers.

It's not unusual for someone to start out at this level. The problem happens when you *stay* there.

I was on a radio call-in talk show recently when a man called in who sounded to me to be a very "motivated" kind of a person. During the conversation, I asked the man, on the air, if he was in network marketing. His answer was, *"Well, kind of . . ."* I then asked the man his name. He said he'd rather not give it out on the air.

What an incredible opportunity that man missed! There were more than *twenty-five thousand people* listening to that broadcast—and all of them were in that man's hometown. I would have given his telephone number out over the air, and referred all those listeners to him as a network marketing resource in their area, if he had only followed my lead. If only he had not been a member of the silent corps of Stealth Distributors, he could have given a major boost to his business with his *one phone call* to that radio show!

Stealth Distributors live in the shadows of their own dreams—never quite willing to truly commit, never willing to take a final stand for their own futures.

There are times to talk proudly about your association with Amway, and there are times to remain quiet—choosing to wait for the appropriate time to prospect or to show the plan. But some people *always* remain quiet, politely waiting for a better opportunity that will never come.

Chances for success:
If timidity, or uncertainty causes you to hold back, that uncertainty can do nothing but keep you from reaching the exact goals in your future that you so badly want to reach.

There is no one who is a Ruby, or an Emerald, or a Diamond today, who allows his old programs of self-induced silence to stop him. If you are afraid to stand up and be proud of what you believe in, you cannot succeed.

Recommendations:
Begin getting rid of every old program you have that questions your success. Start practicing the new programs now, every chance you get.

And take the chance. It is a safe risk. Follow the plan to the letter. Talk to people, and learn to share the dream. Follow every step. Trust it, and do it.

You don't have to be a glib salesperson, an experienced presenter, or a movie star. Quite the opposite. You just have to follow the plan. And every chance you get, with your new Self-Talk, start creating new internal programs, *within yourself*, that build your self-belief. The plan will not let you down. With more of the right programs, neither will you.

PICTURE #2: "THE DOUBTING THOMAS"

Basic operating style: *I would like to believe this, but . . .*

The word "doubt" means nothing more than a mixture of uncertainty and fear.

If you are an Amway Distributor, there are only two kinds of doubt that could be holding you back. The first doubt says, *"Can it work?"* The answer to that one is clear: *"Yes, it can."* It's working every day. And it's working for a lot of people who may be a lot less equipped than you are.

The second doubt says, *"Can I do it?"*

The answer to that question is up to your old programs and what you decide to do right now. The real answer is, *"Yes, without a doubt, you* can *do it!"*

Doubting Thomases are people who want to make it work, but they let their own insecurities get in the way. They are the people who would like to reach the other side of the ravine, but they are afraid to jump more than part of the way across.

Chances for success:

I have not met a single Diamond who is a Doubting Thomas. Neither have I met a single Ruby or an Emerald who lets doubt play any part in his or her success. A simple rule to follow is: *Diamonds don't doubt.*

Recommendations:

Choose to have faith. If you doubt the program, listen to your sponsor, and every successful person above you and around you. The truth is, the more you know about Amway, and the more you practice the plan, the more faith you will have.

If you doubt *yourself,* work on changing the programs you have that cause you to have the doubts in the first place. If I could change your programs, I could take away every doubt you have that has ever held you back, by giving you the right new Self-Talk to focus on. You can do that.

PICTURE #3: "THE PROCRASTINATOR"

Basic operating style: *I'll get started later.*

We have all met them. We have all had it happen to us. As one network marketer I talked to recently said, "I really want to do this. I'll get started sometime soon."

Have you ever thought about how many things you intended to do this year—or for the past *five* years—that you didn't do?

When I meet a network marketer—and I meet a lot of them—I often ask the question, *"Are you doing it?"* I am still amazed at the number of those people whose response is almost the same: *"I haven't really gotten started yet . . . but I'm going to—soon."*

The procrastinator is the "Going-To." They like the *idea* of being successful, but they have a problem getting there. Usually that's because they don't have enough belief within themselves to get them started. Beyond that, is almost always nothing more than their old programs of disbelief or indifference that pull them down—so they fail to take the everyday business steps it takes to get them there.

Procrastination is always one of the clearest signs of negative programming. Those are programs that lead to some form of giving up, or giving in. If you are putting things off, if you aren't doing what you know you could do—what are the programs you have, right now, that are stopping you?

Chances for success:

The procrastinator can never succeed. If you put things off until later, you're putting off your success until then, too.

Recommendations:

Find the programs that cause you to put things off, and change them. Usually it is either fear, or doubt, or a lack of self-belief, that causes procrastination. Don't worry about the procrastination. Work on the programs. Pay special attention to the Self-Talk script in Chapter Eight entitled, **"I Take Action Now!"** *Then do it.*

PICTURE #4: "THE NO-DIRECTION DYNAMO"

Basic operating style: *Lots of ambition—little focus.*

These distributors are not necessarily skyrocketing toward success. Well . . . right *now* they are. But tomorrow they won't be. And the next day . . . they will be again!

This is the picture of network marketers who aren't quite sure where they're going. One day they're in. The next day they're not. And tomorrow, or next week . . . well, who knows?

They have great potential, but they aren't quite sure where they're going. Their intentions are great. But *their programs* are working against them.

They're the kind of distributor who always seems to have plenty of energy and enthusiasm, but often never really gets anywhere.

Most of them fall away in time—but not because they lacked courage; they had never learned how to set a course that would help them reach one incredible goal. They're not focused enough to aim at one star in their heavens. They want them all, and wind up reaching none of them.

If you know people like this, don't be too hard on them. None of us tries to be unsure or unfocused. It's only our old programs that set us up, and toss us and turn us from one goal to another, and from one direction to the next.

The No-Direction Dynamos are not powerless people, lacking the courage they need to support their convictions. They possess all the personal power they need; they're just not sure what their convictions *are.* Their lives have all the promise of a dazzling sunrise—except there is no sun.

They are, for the moment, enthusiastic about Amway, but

they feel equally compelled to follow the next new idea that comes along. They go first one direction, and then the next, because they lack the *self*-direction they need to give clear-cut definition to their lives.

These are intelligent, goal-seeking missiles. They are potentially powerful and effective. But they are aiming their lives into the future—indiscriminately—at an invisible map of unknown targets, and wondering why they are not hitting the mark.

Chances for success:

If you don't find your focus, you lose. But you have all of the energy it takes to succeed. If you find the *right* focus—you win.

Recommendations:

Focus. Use Self-Talk—a lot of it—to focus and refocus daily. Follow the plan. Get a picture of the dream. And then focus again. Talk to your sponsor about this, and don't hold back. Write your goals down on paper, and keep them simple, achievable, and direct. And then focus again. The Army and Navy do that. Good colleges and universities do that. Fortune 500 companies do that. Churches do that. Diamonds do that. All truly successful people do that.

There are no accidental successes in Amway. If you want to get there, you have to *focus*.

PICTURE #5: "THE OVERNIGHT SUCCESS"

Basic operating style: *I don't need to follow the plan.*

There are Diamonds in Amway who have risen rapidly to the top. But not one of them has done it overnight. When you do something this important, and follow the rules, it takes time to do it right. That's why it lasts.

You may turn years into months, now and then, but every Diamond will tell you, "Don't expect to get rich quick." Getting rich, and staying that way, takes a little longer.

Not long ago, I was asked by a radio interviewer how long it took me to write my last book. My answer was, "Fifty-two years, and three-and-a-half months."

You won't have to wait fifty-some years to have your next major success with Amway. But patience, even a little patience, has more than virtue—it is simply intelligent to be willing to follow the plan, for as long as it takes—and make it *work.*

There is a bottom line to this one: There is no such thing as *get rich quick.* There is no magical overnight success. That isn't how life works. We know that.

If now and then you meet someone who is having trouble making his car payments today, and expects to be a millionaire tomorrow, that's okay. He has the right to live with his programs. Just take care of yours.

If you want to be a millionaire, or do anything else equally incredible, earn it. If you want to earn it, follow the plan.

You may not do it overnight. But one day, and it may not be too long from now, you will remember the moment you chose to take this seriously, follow the plan, and make it work. When you get there, it may seem like you did it overnight. For now, follow the plan.

Chances for success:
There is no magic. Amway is not now, nor has it ever been,

a way to get rich quick. But it is a very stable and reliable way to become wealthy in the right way. (And that means a lot more than just financial success.)

Recommendations:

If you believe in becoming an overnight success, obtain and use Self-Talk programs that build self-esteem, create focus, and help you set goals. Wealth is the result of a state of mind. Creating that state of mind will help you get the real thing—and hold onto it for the rest of your life.

PICTURE #6: "THE SILENT PARTNER"

Basic operating style: *The "quiet person" on the team.*

I believe that most "silent partners" help us. That partner could be a wife, or a husband, or someone else who is very close to us. Some of these people might try to pull you away from your interest in Amway, but the silent one will usually wait it out, to see what you will do.

People who are quiet are usually more analytical than others. They tend toward logic, practical values, and common sense. There are a lot of these quieter people who are very successful Amway Distributors.

There are many people among us who are there—strong, quiet, intelligent, and watching—but they are more the presence behind the throne, than they are the spokespersons for our dreams.

Chances for success:

Excellent chances for success. The people who are always

the most outspoken are not always the most successful. Listen to the quiet ones. They are *listening* while the rest of the world is talking.

Recommendations:

If you are the quiet one, and you would like to be more outgoing, learning the right Self-Talk can help. Meanwhile, do your best to let your husband, wife, or partner know what you think and how you feel. If you don't express it, the other person may not know it.

Next, look at the details of the information you get from the people in your organization. Look at the logic of the plan. It's okay to be cautious, but don't live your life holding yourself back.

You're intelligent. If you were going to invest in a new stock offering, you would research the investment, get all the input you could, figure the odds, and make your investment. Take Amway just as seriously as a major investment. But once you've decided to do it, don't pull your bet. Get behind it and make it work.

PICTURE #7: "THE TEAM PLAYER"

Basic operating style: *The Distributor Every Sponsor Dreams Of.*

Look for team players. Surround yourself with people who excel at making teamwork work. Sponsor these people into Amway. They will thank you—and you will thank them. Team players follow rules, work the plan, join teams and build teams, motivate, support and encourage every player on the team, and want to win the biggest and best prizes there are.

The team player's psychological profile is perfect for building your success. Add the Amway plan to that list of attributes and you have a win/win in the making.

Chances for success:

Work with this one. You cannot lose. This person will be there when you need him, he will listen, learn, follow the steps, make it work, and be your friend for life.

If you are a true team player yourself, you already know what to do. But you are part of the most important team in the field. Stay on the team. Build it. And expect to win.

Recommendations:

The Self-Talk a team player needs most is the Self-Talk of recognition and reward. If you are one of these fine players yourself, you should do two things. First, reward everyone else on your team. They worked with you to make things work. They're the team you count on, and you have to let them know it. Then, reward yourself.

PICTURE #8: "THE PLAN FOLLOWER"

Basic operating style: *Does it right; cannot lose . . .*

This is the ultimate Amway Distributor. This is the one who makes it work. You can find yourself in any of the other snapshots of network marketers in this chapter, but unless you find yourself here, you may never find yourself there—in the sky, or on the stage—with those Diamonds around you.

I understand that, as an Amway Distributor, you are told to work the plan. It is simple. It works. And anyone who is willing to follow the plan can succeed.

That is a message you've heard many times. Even from my outside viewpoint of motivational psychology, the concept of Amway, and the plan they have given you, make sense.

But it was interesting to discover how true the concept is in practice. Every single Diamond I interviewed, in some way, said exactly the same thing. Above everything else they did, they became Diamonds by *following the plan*.

Chances of success:
This one is simple. If you don't do it, you won't "get there." If you follow the plan, and stay with it, you will.

Recommendations:
Work the plan.

If you got that same message a hundred times a day, it would not be too much. If you were meant to be anything less than the true achiever that you are, you would not even be reading these words.

This message is for you. Work the plan.

Tonight, the last thought you think, make the choice to work the plan. Live it, dream it, believe in it, and make it happen. Go ahead. Right now. Just to yourself. Say "I work the plan." If you say it so often you can't help but believe it, then you'll make it happen.

PICTURE #9: "THE POSITIVE DREAMER"

Basic operating style: *The incredible "can do" Distributor.*

Some of us are inspired to achieve. I will never forget the day my wife Bonnie and I were driving down a beautiful highway on a Sunday morning, and because we were traveling, and couldn't attend service, she put a "Dreamer" CD into the disk player in our van.

I had recently spoken at an Amway function in another city, and while we were there, we had acquired our first-ever Dreamer CDs. As we listened, we were more than "inspired." The music and the message affected both of us in an exceptional way—so much so that I made it a point to pick up the telephone a few days later, and place a call to someone who had helped to make that music possible. I wanted to thank him.

Mark Smith started out making music, singing with a group. In time, the group he sang with renamed themselves "Dreamer," and at about the same time, Dreamer became a demand vocal group at major Amway events nationwide. (If you can see Dreamer in person, you should. If you can't, you should get some of their CDs and play them loudly. They will inspire you.)

Having met the members of the group in person, it is clear that each of them, in his own fashion, shared the dream—and now they share the dream with other Amway members everywhere, every chance they get.

As the name of that inspiring singing group implies, to make it work, you have to dream the dream. And that is the point. To move mountains, *you have to have the dream.*

The Positive Dreamer is the distributor who sees the picture so clearly that he never gives up. This is the network marketer who refuses to listen to the old programs that try to stop him; he is too busy building, and listening to, the *new* programs that help him succeed.

Chances for success:

If you want to see it in your life, you're going to have to see it in your mind. That's called dreaming, and it's essential to doing anything well. If you learn to dream, and take positive action every day, your chances for success are great.

Recommendations:

Go ahead. Believe in the dream. Why would you want to do anything less? Of course, you have to work the plan. But people who dream of their futures in their minds always do better than people who fail to dream at all.

Your dream creates the belief that inspires every action you will take.

Your dream creates the richness of the soil in which all your seeds are planted. Whatever grows, will be the result of your dream.

Your dream creates the focus, and gives you the picture of your own unlimited future.

Your dream creates the road you follow—and gives you the reason to follow that road.

Your dream gives you a reason to wake up every morning, and live a life that most people can only dream of living.

Your dream is the future you are creating for yourself, right now.

People who have a clear picture of the dream have a very good chance of achieving it. If you want to succeed, you have to dream. If you want to dream, you have to believe in yourself. If you want to have more belief in yourself, change your programs. The key here is to work on self-belief, every day. The dreams will follow.

PICTURE #10: THE "STARBOUND" DISTRIBUTOR

Basic operating style: *The one who makes everything work.*

What a great gift to *everyone's* life, this person is!

The Starbound Distributor is the one we would like to be most like. This Amway Distributor is the Diamond in the making. Whether you are just beginning, or almost there, this is the Pearl, the Ruby, the Emerald, the *gem.*

This is the person to find, to support, to duplicate, and to emulate—this is the one to recreate.

If you, yourself, are Starbound—if you are on your way—I applaud you and encourage you. What you are doing now is of greater importance than anything else you might ever do in your life.

Chances for success:

For most people, this *is* success! Learn to emulate one of these winners, and the future you are creating will not let you down.

Recommendations:

If you are one of those special people already, whatever you are doing, keep doing it. If you are not yet a "Starbound" Distributor, find one, follow suit, and learn everything you can. If you are not already following a clearly-defined, written-out goal plan to go Diamond, consider doing that now.

Your final objective should be to excel in everything you do. That is what a Starbound person does. That is what makes successful people, and Direct Distributors, and Pearls, and Rubies, and Emeralds, and Diamonds.

And if you follow a few very simple steps, that is exactly what *you* can do.

*"The number one thing
that will ever try to stop you
is fear.*

*Imagine a future
without the fear.*

*If you can get past the fear,
the only thing left
in front of you
will be your own bright
future."*

Chapter Eleven
Overcoming The #1 Problem

s I researched the attitudes of successful network marketers, there was one question, beyond any other, that needed an answer. That question was: What is the single biggest problem people have while they're trying to reach success? *What is the one problem, more than any other, that slows people down, or stops them completely?*

I am not surprised that I got the same answer time and again. The answer is a universal truth. Topping the list of things that stop people from doing their best in network marketing is the exact same problem that stops people from achieving in *any* field.

The #1 thing that will ever try to stop you is *fear*.

It is fear that could have stopped you from saying *"Yes!"* to the opportunity of network marketing in the first place. It is fear that can stop you from making the next phone call, or setting the next appointment. It is fear that can cause you to put off showing the plan to even the most promising new prospect. It is fear that can stop the next person you make a presentation to, from saying "yes" to you, and in so doing, miss the opportunity of a lifetime. It is fear that can cause you to think that it will never pay off for you . . . and on, and on.

IF YOU GET PAST THE FEAR, YOU CAN DO ANYTHING

As one Diamond told me, "If we could just teach our distributors how to overcome fear, nothing in this world could stop us from reaching every goal we set."

Imagine a future without the fear. If you can get past the fear, the only thing left in front of you will be your own bright future.

Fear causes us to hesitate, to avoid following through, to see the problem instead of the solution, or to believe in the worst instead of expecting the best.

The standard advice most of us have gotten is to be told the old adage again about having ". . . nothing to fear but fear itself."

That may be true, but it doesn't do much good when you've had your eighth "no" in a row, and your best friend thinks you're crazy for wasting your time, and it's been a long week and you're tired, and the telephone just sits and looks at you and dares you to make one more call and get rejected again. At that moment we never consciously think to ourselves, "I think I'll stop because I'm *afraid* to go on," and yet it is fear in one of its most cleverly-disguised forms that will cause us to shake our head, turn out the light, and tell ourselves we'll get the job done some other time.

We have often been told that the single most important attribute for success is dogged determination—refusing to stop, no matter what. So how do you fit these two opposing forces together? *Determination* and *hesitation* do not make good bedfellows!

There is one source of fear that is the healthy kind—the kind that keeps us out of trouble, protects us, and keeps us alive. But we're not talking about that kind of fear here.

WHAT OUR PROGRAMS OF FEAR SOUND LIKE

The kind of fear that stops us from succeeding—or ever getting started—is the kind of fear caused by old mental programs. Those programs tell us:

What we cannot do.

How tough it's going to be.

We're not good enough.

We wouldn't know how to act or what to say.

If we do "get lucky" and get successful—something bad will happen and we'll lose it anyway.

We don't deserve to be that successful.

What will other people think?

Other people have a better chance than I do . . . etc., etc.

Or a thousand other unconscious programs that have us spending more time *doubting* ourselves than *believing* in ourselves.

I know there are times when you haven't been so sure about yourself. I know there can be all sorts of reasons for you to think that you'll never have all the riches and joys and freedom that some people achieve. But what if none of those reasons is *true*? What if the real truth about you is much better than you have ever imagined?

Let me tell you the real truth about you.

THE REAL TRUTH ABOUT YOU

- You can do it. You don't have to wait. You don't have to hesitate. You don't have to put anything off. There is no better time for you to take action and get moving.

- If you have ever had any fears in the past, today is a good time to put them behind you. You don't have to let anything at all stop you. You're better than that! Besides, you deserve better than that.

- The only difference between you and someone who has

already gotten there is the time it takes to do it. So why not take the time? Go for it! There's nothing stopping you. All you have to do is believe in yourself, right now, today . . . and never, ever stop believing in yourself.

- Anytime an old fear tries to come back, tell it its time is over. You're in control now. You're calling the shots. You're choosing your own future and you're doing something about it.

- You know that fear and hesitation are nothing more than forgetting who you really are, what you really can do. So go ahead. You can get past the fear, if you remind yourself of the truth.

- If you'd like to have freedom in your life, you can.

- If you'd like to be financially free and secure, you will be.

- If you'd like to have independence, call your own shots, and have the freedom to choose for yourself, you'll have it.

- If you'd like to be the best, kindest, most caring and loving husband or wife there has ever been, you can be.

- If you'd like to be the kind of parent who nurtures, teaches, inspires, and leads, and have the time to do that in your own family, you can.

- If you'd like to strengthen your faith, live up to your values, and share that faith and those values with others, you will.

- If you'd like to learn, to grow, to expand your horizons, increase your knowledge, and improve your mind, your life, and your future, all you have to do is choose.

- If you would like to live a life filled with value and worth, you most certainly can.

- All you have to do is be yourself. You have everything it takes.

- You have the desire, the drive, the ambition, and the dream.

- You have the opportunity, the tools, and the time to make it happen.

- You have the intelligence to learn everything you need to know, and to put what you already know into action.

- You never, for a single moment, let fear or hesitation get in your way. Why? Because you are a winner!

- You were born to succeed. You've got the ability, the attitude, the endurance, and the belief.

- Add what you've already got to a group of people around you—an incredible network of champions—who are there to see you through, and you will one day be one of those diamonds in the sky!

NOW GIVE THAT MESSAGE TO YOURSELF

If I could talk to you for even a few minutes each day, or if we could sit down for a moment or two when things aren't going just right, or when some old fear or doubt creeps back in, I think I could convince you, in no uncertain terms, just how good you really are.

So for now, here's what it feels like to do that for yourself.

Read those same words again. But this time, if you can, read them out loud—or at least, read them very strongly; be consciously aware of what they say. This time, the truth about you will be said to you—*by you*. Read the following message to *you!* Enjoy the truth. This is you:

I can do it. I don't have to wait. I don't have to hesitate. I don't have to put anything off. There is no better time for me to take action and get moving.

If I have ever had any fears in the past, today is a good time to put them behind me. I don't have to let anything at all stop me. I'm better than that! Besides, I deserve better than that.

The only difference between me and someone who has already gotten there is the time it takes to do it. So I might as well take the time. I'm going for it! There's nothing stopping me. All I have to do is believe in myself, right now, today . . . and never, ever stop believing in myself.

Anytime an old fear tries to come back, I tell it its time is over. I'm in control now. I'm calling the shots. I'm choosing my own future and I'm doing something about it.

144

I know that fear and hesitation are nothing more than forgetting who I really am—what I really can do. So I go ahead. I remind myself of the truth, and I get past the fear.

If I'd like to have freedom in my life, I can.

If I'd like to be financially free and secure, I will be.

If I'd like to have independence, call my own shots, and have the freedom to choose for myself, I'll have it.

If I'd like to be the best, kindest, most caring and loving husband or wife there has ever been, I can be.

If I'd like to be the kind of parent who nurtures, teaches, inspires, and leads, and have the time to do that in my own family, I can.

If I'd like to strengthen my faith, live up to my values, and share that faith and those values with others, I will.

If I'd like to learn, to grow, to expand my horizons, increase my knowledge, and improve my mind, my life, and my future, all I have to do is choose.

Because I would like to live a life filled with value and worth, I most certainly can.

All I have to do is be myself. I have everything it takes. I have the desire, I have the drive, I have the ambition, and I have the dream.

I have the opportunity, the tools, and I make the time to

make it happen.

I have the intelligence to learn everything I need to know, and to put what I already know into action.

I never, for a single moment, let fear or hesitation get in my way. Why? Because I am a winner!

I was born to succeed. I've got the ability, the attitude, the endurance, and the belief.

Add what I already have to a group of people around me—an incredible Network of Champions—who are there to see me through, and I will one day be one of those diamonds in the sky!

Does that declaration of your refusal to let fear live in your life—stated in that way—sound familiar? It should. It is a form of new Self-Talk, of the highest order.

The right Self-Talk, when combined with a positive goal that moves you forward, *replaces fear!* In time, enough of the right kind of Self-Talk will get *rid* of the programs that *caused* the fear in the first place.

Go ahead. Set your goal, decide where you want to go, and start replacing the old programs of fear that have been holding you back. Put your fear aside; refuse to let it in. Have faith; pray; work the plan; and *never give up.* Most of the fear will go away if you focus on your goal, and concentrate on *moving forward.*

*"When you are faced
with opposition
from someone who should
know better,
remember the phrase:*

*'I no longer live my life
by the negative opinions
of others.'"*

Chapter Twelve

When Your Family Doesn't Understand

L et's assume that by now, *you're* convinced that network marketing can work for you, and that Amway is where you want to be. But what do you do if your *in-home* team isn't working like it should be?

It is easy to see that network marketing is designed to create *team success*—especially at *home*. Husband, wife, and family Amway teams dominate the rolls of successful network marketers. But the two people in the marriage, or in the relationship, don't always see everything eye to eye, and the sacrifices each of them has to make are not always accepted with equal enthusiasm.

Maybe the husband doesn't mind giving up his evenings and his weekends to the new "family business," but what if his wife doesn't agree? Or maybe it's the wife who sees their new business as the breakthrough she's been praying for . . .

but her husband still spends more time sitting in front of the television set than making calls or showing the plan.

When I meet and talk to couples after a public speaking engagement, I can always spot the "Amway couples." They have that special look. But even among them, I have often noticed that their enthusiasm is not always equally matched.

Sometimes it is the husband who crowds in close, reaching out to shake hands with me, or to hand me a book to sign; while the wife hangs back, looking more like she is there to get him home on time than to get remotivated. Or it may be the woman who is sparkling with positive electricity, and the man who doesn't yet have "the glow of impending success."

HOW DO YOU MAKE IT WORK TOGETHER?

If teamwork works better than working at odds, how can two of you, especially in a marriage or close relationship, make sure you are pulling together and not apart?

One Diamond recently told me how his own wife, at first, didn't believe they could make Amway work. She had gone along with him, sat through the presentation, and even agreed that there wouldn't be any harm in just trying it. But she remained skeptical, even when her husband started working the plan himself. She wasn't dead-set against it, but she wasn't very supportive either.

"What did you do to convince her?" I asked him. After all, the two were now Diamonds. Something had changed.

"I just kept doing it," the husband replied. "And then, before long, it started *working*. There's nothing like success to convince someone that it works!"

But that Diamond may have been luckier than some people. I know other distributors who feel they are fighting a very tough battle, *up hill,* and they are fighting it *alone.* For them, the toughest thing they have to overcome is the negative attitude of the person they are living with.

What do you do if the person you're married to is negative, or doesn't feel like *you* do? Your life in network marketing should make your marriage *stronger,* not pull it apart. If you do it right, your life is supposed to get *better,* not worse.

THE OTHER PERSON'S PROGRAMS

It will first help to know that your opinions, your thoughts, your attitude, and your actions—even what you say—are based on the programs you've already gotten. The same is true of the person you're married to. And *you can't* make someone's programs *change,* just because you want them to.

If someone close to you is negative, what you're actually seeing is that person's programs doing what they were designed to do—even if that means being negative, or shy, or disbelieving, or anything else that could be working against you. If the computer in your office is not programmed to do accounting, would you get mad at it every time it refused to balance your checkbook?

But it's not unusual to get upset with someone whose *mental* computer is not programmed to do what you want *it* to do—like agreeing with you and being a super network marketing partner, as an example.

The next time you start to have an argument with your "partner," think to yourself, "How is this person's mental computer *programmed* to think?" Learning to be aware of the other person's programs won't change them, of course. But it sure can help you avoid some heated disagreements. And even more important, knowing that your partner has different programs than you do will help you understand why he or she may not have the same zeal for being successful in Amway as you do. It isn't that person's *fault.* It is that person's *programs.*

WHAT IF YOU WANT TO HELP CHANGE THE OTHER PERSON'S PROGRAMS?

If your partner wants to make some changes (that has to be her, or his, decision), there are some things you can do to help. You can't change the other person's programs *for* him—but you *can* help.

The first step you can take is to change the Self-Talk around your home.

Remember, everything you do, think, say, or *hear,* is a program. So everything your partner hears, even at home, is adding to his or her programs. That means everything you say, at any time, *does* make a difference.

Are your words building the other person up, or pulling the other person down?

Do your comments usually create common pathways that both of you can follow?

Do you really *communicate* or are you just expressing your

opinions? (Your opinions are important, but your opinions are also nothing more than printouts of your *own* past programs.)

START WITH LISTENING . . .
BUT DON'T STOP THERE

If you are changing some of your own programs by listening to Self-Talk tapes, then be sure to listen to those tapes around your home, while the other person is nearby. Self-Talk works best when the tapes are played *quietly*, in the background—almost as if you were just casually overhearing them. As long as they can be heard out loud, your brain is listening—and so is your partner's.

So while you are improving your *own* success programs, your partner will also be getting the same, new set of success programs, just by your playing them at home, in the background.

However, even though I have seen frequent listening create some near-miraculous recoveries from negativity, I would not stop there. Starting a comprehensive program of using Self-Talk techniques may be the basis of good, solid reprogramming, but it should be aided by every positive attitude and motivational tool you have in the Amway arsenal.

Listen to your Amway cassettes faithfully! Those, too, when played when the two of you are together, will train and motivate you, but they will also add to a positive ambience of success in your home—and in your life. Read the books, attend every meeting you can, and make sure you keep yourself surrounded with the most positive, most going-for-it people you know. And then, stay with it and *refuse to stop.*

YOUR MOST IMPORTANT ACTION STEP: WRITE YOUR GOALS *TOGETHER*

As soon as you begin using Self-Talk, and making sure you have exactly the right programs you need to become successful, the most important thing you can do as a couple, is to write your personal and professional goal plan— *together.* You may find it very revealing.

The secret is in going through the steps of identifying your goals together. What you will learn from completing a joint goal plan will tell you a lot about which areas of programs you need to work on—if you want to reach your goals together.

One tool that many people have told me they find especially helpful is the Self-Talk tape entitled "Mastering Your Goals." That is not a traditional goal-setting tape. It is a carefully written and recorded script of Self-Talk programs that help the listeners focus and fine-tune their goals tighter and tighter, each time they listen.

When I am instructing network marketers on how to use this particular tape, I always make it a point to insist that if it is a married couple, they listen to this tape *together.* Why? Because if you are going to define your goals and support them with good Self-Talk, you should be sure your goals are the kind that work *together.* As the old saying accurately tells us: Be careful what you want—you'll probably get it.

If you want to reach the end of the road together, you have to begin by setting goals that put both of you on the *same road* in the first place. If your goals—even your *unconscious* goals—and programs are not consistent with each other's, your chances of getting there together are not worth starting for. But even if you agree to work together, the responsibility for your success, will still be up to *you*.

THE FINAL ANSWER IS:
YOUR SUCCESS WILL BE UP TO YOU

You can help your partner get better. But you cannot change your partner's programs by yourself. Encourage your partner. You are trying to make life better for both of you—for your whole family. Talk about the goals you have together. Paint, and repaint the picture of where you are going, what you are willing to do to get there, and what that journey can mean for both of you.

Become your partner's best *motivator* and biggest *fan.* Show how much *faith* you have in him or in her. Set your goals together, practice Self-Talk, and make sure you both have the right programs. Do everything you can do to strengthen your "team of two," and make it work together.

And then go and look at *yourself* in the mirror again. It will still be up to you.

If you are already blessed with someone in your life who is so supportive and so "with you" that your success is all but insured, you have a lot to be thankful for. Say your prayers of thanksgiving every night, and every day work to make your relationship even stronger.

If there is someone in your life who you would like to be more on the team, prayer can help here, too, but you will have to refuse to give up or give in if you want to succeed.

The point here is that you should become very aware of how important your goal is to you. Someone else's negativity is never a good reason to give up. When you are faced with opposition from someone who should know better, remember the Self-Talk phrase, *"I no longer live my life based on the negative opinions of others."* It may not change the other person's *opinion*, but they won't be able to change your *actions*, either.

Once you have done *everything you can do* to encourage the other person (or people) in your life, if they cannot yet see the light of their own bright futures, you will still have to rely on *you*—to get you there. Meanwhile, the following section should help you give them a picture of what you're trying to do.

AN IMPORTANT MESSAGE TO THE VERY SPECIAL "PARTNER" IN YOUR LIFE

If there is someone in your life who you care about, but who doesn't quite share your dream, what could you—or anyone—say, that would help that one person see the vision of what you see, or feel the excitement that you feel?

I know you can't automatically transfer your greatest hopes to someone else. But if you have chosen to make Amway a key part of your personal growth and your success, then I have a message that I would like to share with those people who are important to you.

They may not choose to read this entire book. In fact, we're talking here about those people who may not presently share your faith in Amway. They may even think you are foolish, or dreaming, or wasting your time. So instead of asking those people to read everything in this book, you may just want to share these few important pages that follow.

The person you're thinking of could be your wife, or it could be your husband. Or it could be someone else in your family. Whoever that person—or those special people—may be, the following message is written just for them:

AN OPEN LETTER TO AMWAY FAMILIES FROM DR. SHAD HELMSTETTER

If someone close to you has asked you to read this, I want you to know I suggested it because I thought it might help.

To begin with, you're a very important person. What you think *counts.* What you do *matters.* What you want *makes a difference.*

If you are a wife, your husband obviously cares about you and he cares about everything you think. And because *you* matter, you should know that how you feel about his goals matters a lot.

If you are a husband, then what you think about your wife's

ideas and directions could have a strong influence on how well your wife does-especially if she wants to find her success-and hopes you will find *your* success-in Amway.

If you are a family member, or close to anyone who wants you to believe in what he or she wants to do in Amway, there are some things you should know.

I'm going to tell you some things you can believe in, because, like you, I am an outsider, looking in. Because I study, and do research, and write about people who learn how to be successful, I can speak honestly about any group of people I research.

I have been studying and writing about people for many years. I long ago learned to recognize the difference between the people and the ideas that were "for real" and could be counted on, and the people whose ideas you could not trust.

This is one of those times when I would ask you to believe. Believe in your husband, or your wife, or that one special friend or family member who wants you to share the very real dream of Amway. They're not asking you to believe in miracles or impossibilities. They are asking you to believe in their future . . . and in *yours.*

Like you and like me, they just want the chance to be someone *special,* to do things *right,* to achieve real, lasting success. They want to have a home, a family, and a future that works. Why would anyone want to suggest they should do anything less?

But this person, this one with the dream, *needs your help.*

And what you *do* next could change what *happens* next.

You could question the dream, and say it can't work. But there are far too many people who have made it work before, to really question it at all.

You could say this one person who needs you now, does not have what it takes. But there are too many other people, with far fewer strengths, and even less determination, who have *already* done it.

You could say that Amway is only a dream, an idea, an impossible picture of success that could not possibly include you. But that dream has turned thousands of lives from hopeless mediocrity to endless, life-changing opportunities. And that could include you. If you support that dream, you could find that *it isn't a dream at all*. It is you, and your family, and your future.

There is one very important person in your life who would like you to be a part of the team that helps make your life work-better than most people could ever imagine. This picture of you, and the people you care about, living a better life-this picture is *real*. It is being lived by a lot of people just like you, right now. All they did was to agree to succeed. Instead of saying *"No"* to that incredible future in front of them, they just said *"Yes."*

That doesn't mean that once you say *"Yes,"* everything thereafter will be free. No one would want or expect that. But from the moment you commit to working for that future-let's call it the "Amway future"-your future will change.

Having studied Amway, and its exceptional people, I believe that if you follow the simple steps that others before you have proven so well, if you do just that-and *keep doing it*-your own future will change. Your life could end up being more safe, and more financially secure, and uplifting, and in control, and more exciting and rewarding than you had ever imagined it could be.

Now, for a moment, I'll ask you to consider the *opposite.*

What if *none* of those dreams I have just described to you could ever come true? After all, you *do* have the right to choose any direction you want to take with your life. You can agree, disagree, support and give life, or withhold your support, and take that future away.

Imagine a world without the belief that one, or two people together, can reach the highest limits of their potential. For just a moment, take the husband who wants so badly to achieve. Instead of seeing him set goals, reach for his true success, spend his days, some of his evenings, and even some weekends doing what it takes to make his life work, let's look at the opposite.

Let's say he *doesn't* stay with Amway. He's discouraged, or you or someone else convinces him he isn't capable of reaching the dream Amway offers to his future.

In so doing, you, or someone else, successfully reduces his future to little more than a constant replay of a past that doesn't work. In time, the incredible future that could have been his-and yours-is no longer a true future at all. In time, that dream, that exciting potential, that future, like a meteor ablaze in the nighttime sky, dies out. And finally, because *no one helped*-because no one *believed*-the glimmer of light that was the fire of belief goes out.

Without the dream, without the goal, the incredible, wonderful dreamer-the achiever-changes. Without your belief, without your trust, he returns once again to what he was *before* he had that dream.

A man without a dream is like the man who spends endless evenings at home, sitting in front of the television set, watching TV in the same way that he moves through life-switching from channel to channel to channel, hoping something better will come along, and somehow knowing nothing ever will.

That's a picture you would never want-but *it doesn't have to be that way.* You can help keep the dream alive.

If you care about the one in your life who is trying to make your life better, there are three things you could do, and should do, that will help, more than you might ever know.

The three things you can do, right now, are:

Give *strength* to the one who strives to succeed.
Give *belief* to the one who gives life to his dreams.
Give *courage* to the one who dares to change.

What you do next will make a difference.

SOME ACTIONS YOU CAN TAKE RIGHT NOW
THAT WILL HELP

Once, many years ago, my two young sons were discussing with their mother and me what they should do with their lives. I believe I surprised their mother, and probably delighted my sons, when I advised both of those two young boys to one day, *"get on the next ship leaving the harbor, sail the greatest seas, and make your life a grand adventure!"*

Today, many years later, both of those young boys have grown into young men. One of them has climbed to the highest peaks of Machu Picchu in the Andes; the other has climbed uncharted peaks in computer technology. Neither of them is worse for the wear—or the expectation. Both of them are exceptional human beings. I would, however, hate to think what they might have done, if both of them had just stayed home and watched television.

If you have someone in your life who wants to get better—to achieve, to be more successful—I encourage you to do everything you can to help him or her do it. If, on the other hand, you are one of those who would like to find the support of someone else to help you reach more of the stars in your heavens, I encourage you to ask for that person's support.

You can't change the other person's *programs* by demanding, wanting, or asking. But for a time, if you do it very carefully, you could get the *support* you need to prove how well Amway can work for both of you.

Here are some objectives and action steps that can get you started now.

Objective #1: To create a "team."

You should begin here, even if that team is just two people—you and your wife, or husband, or the significant other person in your life.

Objective #2: To make sure both (or all) of you have the right programs to work with.

Start, right now, an all-out campaign to get rid of the programs that are holding you back, and start building the programs that will end up creating your new success.

Action Step #1:

If there is someone you want to join you on your path to success, ask them to read, as a personal note, the open letter I've included above.

Action Step #2:

After that person has read the words and thought through the ideas, the two of you should discuss the following:

A. Becoming a team, and doing this together.

B. What each of you wants to achieve.

C. What each of you is willing to do to reach the goal.

D. Immediately going to work on creating the kind of programs that will help you succeed—*together*.

YOU HAVE THE RIGHT TO ACHIEVE

If, in the past, you haven't had all the support you'd like to have had to make certain the Amway business would work for you, I encourage you to not give up hope. You are just getting started.

Have courage. Have faith. Believe in your convictions. Prove to the world around you—especially the ones you care about most—that *you* are in control of your future. Don't stop. Don't give up. Don't let *anyone* convince you that you cannot reach your goals.

Remember, you *are* special. You deserve to succeed. No one other than *you* will ever be *you*. No one can ever think or dream *for* you. You have the right to *achieve* in your life—and no one can ever take that right from you. You are going for *real* success—and no one can take that goal from you.

If you want your wife, or your husband, or a family member, or your best friend to join you, but they haven't yet gotten the picture, don't worry too much about that.

Present the plan, show the picture of what you—and they—can do, and *never give up.*

Eventually, everyone will agree with you that when you joined Amway you did the right thing.

One day soon, when you are amazingly successful, and spending the winter relaxing in the sun on an island somewhere, even your most discouraging associates and acquaintances will be happy to share your success with you.

When someone has to call you to wish you "Merry Christmas" when you're on an island in the Caribbean, it is very difficult for them to tell you your dream did not work.

*"Self-Esteem
does not mean 'self-love,'
false pride,
or an arrogant ego.*

*Self-Esteem means
your complete picture
of yourself—
and everything you believe
to be true about you."*

Chapter Thirteen

Building Stronger Self-Esteem

What is your opinion of yourself? If you're going to succeed in the Amway business (or in *anything* worthwhile, for that matter), you're going to have to have good, healthy self-esteem. And we now know that if you don't already *have* it, you *can get* it.

What do you really think about who you are and what you're doing? If you could have the best, true picture of yourself, and your work, what would it look like? How is your faith? How is your belief? Are you set up to succeed?

This idea of having better "self-esteem" has often been misunderstood. Self-esteem, in its classical form, does not mean self-love, false pride, or an arrogant ego. In fact, it really means the opposite of all that. The term "self-esteem" actually means your complete, composite picture of yourself and who you are. Your self-esteem is the *picture* of who you *believe* yourself to be.

This "picture" you have of yourself is important for two reasons:

1. Your self-esteem is always the result of the programs you have about your *self*, right now.

2. Your programmed self-esteem always determines what you end up believing about yourself. What you believe about yourself, unconsciously, always determines what you do.

So if your personal—and business—self-esteem programs are not giving you the best pictures of who you *really are*, and what you can *really accomplish*, those programs will hold you back. We almost always rise to the limits of our self-esteem. If that limit is low, that is, if your picture of yourself is less than the best, than that is what you are likely to achieve.

In the same way, your internal self-esteem programs that make up what you think and how you feel about network marketing, and about Amway in particular, determine most of the choices you make in your business. You have programs about that, and those programs are very real.

The result is, you have a personal sense of self-esteem, and you have a business, or *networking* self-esteem.

LOOK AT THE *"NETWORKING SELF-ESTEEM"* OF THE PEOPLE AROUND YOU

Look around you, at your network associates, and you will

see that this is true.

Some of your friends have that incredible, internal sense of self-acceptance and self-belief. They are the ones who seem to always be motivated. They work hard, they have a goal, they follow the plan, they are almost always optimistic, they help and encourage others, and they refuse to stop.

That kind of attitude is not born of blind acceptance. That kind of positive self-belief comes from some very strong programs of self-esteem—both *personal* self-esteem, and *networking* self-esteem.

Now look at other people you know. They may even be in your organization, but these people are the *other* kind—the kind that is not winning. They are the ones who are "down" on almost everything. They are negative; they have no enthusiasm, and they don't believe in their own success.

It really isn't their fault—it's their *self-esteem*. They have no faith in the business because they have no faith in *themselves*. Their own poor self-esteem is creating a future of failure, and they don't even understand what's happening to them.

We have learned that all self-esteem is "acquired," or imprinted—that is, it is *learned*. Your self-esteem is recorded in an unending series of imprints, or neurological "recordings" in your brain. Layer by layer, recording by recording, your beliefs about yourself are built.

In the brain itself, the process is chemical and it is complicated. But to simplify this process, as we said earlier, just keep in mind that every message you ever receive is recorded in chemical pathways—neuron highways in the brain.

IF YOU CREATE NEW PROGRAMS—
YOU BUILD NEW SELF-ESTEEM

What that means for you right now is that everything you have ever heard, thought, said, or believed, about yourself, and everything you have ever believed about network marketing—and Amway—has been *recorded*, in *neural pathways*, in your brain. Whatever those recordings—those *messages*—have been, unless you have done something to change them, *those programmed "recordings" are still there.*

So when I recommend using some new Self-Talk to create a team of new messages—new programs—to help you, I hope you know that what you are doing is a great deal more scientific that just telling yourself to think a little differently. This isn't just "positive thinking," or anything that simple, or short-lived.

What we're really talking about is *you* taking responsibility for the entire process of your own programming. That means you are in charge of the next programs you get. In the past, this "programming process" has been up to the world around you. From now on, your programming is up to you.

SOME EXCEPTIONAL NEW PROGRAMS
THAT WILL HELP YOU WIN

The following Self-Talk scripts, like each of the scripts in this book, have been written specifically for you. But they also follow some very important rules. Good Self-Talk—the *right* Self-Talk—has to be simple. It has to be direct, and easy to use. And it has to meet specific programming rules that govern its imagery, content, format, and phrasing.

Like every carefully compiled and successful Self-Talk script, the end result is disarmingly simple. Good Self-Talk combines the value of timeless truth, with an almost rhythmic pentameter of poetic verse.

But good Self-Talk, like the following examples, is much more than the right words, written in exactly the right way. This is the kind of Self-Talk that will do more than motivate you. *It is designed to help you replace old programs with something better.*

POSITIVE AMWAY SELF-ESTEEM

You could read and reread the following Self-Talk script only occasionally. Or you could learn the Self-Talk word for word, and memorize it. Or you can listen to it on cassettes, and get the same programs more often, which is what I do myself when there is an area of my life that I want to improve.

You could, of course, choose to read this Self-Talk just this once . . . and then move on.

But I encourage you to take this Self-Talk—these programs—more seriously than that. The words in the following Self-Talk scripts are simple enough. But the meaning, and the *new programs* these words create—with repeated use—are especially important!

It has been my experience that when programs like these become an automatic and natural part of your life, your life becomes automatically and naturally better.

However you feel about *yourself,* and about your role in *network marketing,* right now, imagine hearing these words—getting these same programs—every morning for the next few weeks, or for the next few *months* of your life:

SPECIAL AMWAY DISTRIBUTOR SELF-TALK SCRIPT #4:

"I AM PROUD TO BE IN AMWAY"

I am proud to be in Amway. I like being successful, and being with Amway is the successful way to be.

I like myself, and I like what I am doing with my life.

While I am changing my own life, for the better, I am changing the lives of others . . . for the better.

Because of my work with Amway, I am changing <u>my</u> life, by helping other people change <u>their</u> lives.

Right now, at this moment, and for all the time to come, I take full, and personal responsibility for the success of my dreams.

Amway is growing stronger every day, and with it, I am growing stronger too. I believe in Amway, and Amway believes in me.

If I have ever had any doubts about myself, in the past, I choose to get rid of those doubts forever.

170

I have chosen to be one of the best. I have made the choice to make Amway work in my life. I like what I'm doing . . . and I choose to succeed.

I am proud of what Amway means for me, for my family, and for my life. I am proud I made this choice.

I believe in myself . . . and I believe in Amway.

I have faith that I will be successful in every positive way. I believe it, I work at it, and I make it happen.

I surround myself with the most positive people on this earth. To me, Amway is an incredible family of positive friends.

My home, my family, my work, and my faith are all enhanced by the positive enrichment that Amway brings to my life.

I am proud to be a part of changing the world in a positive way.

I am improving my own life while I am helping others improve theirs.

I am proud—incredibly proud to be a part of the Amway team. It is the most exciting, worthwhile, most winning team on earth.

I am proud to be in Amway!

Imagine listening to that one Self-Talk script each morning when you wake up—or reading through it out loud as you start your day!

When you are proud of who you are, and what you're doing, your enthusiasm shows. Your self-esteem quotient goes up. And you begin to think about doing better.

Imagine having that kind of belief in Amway the next time you meet someone new, or the next time you show the plan!

If you want other people to believe, your belief has to come from within. When you make that kind of Self-Talk a permanent part of who you are, you are literally *creating* that belief within you.

ANOTHER SELF-TALK PROGRAM
THAT TELLS IT LIKE IT IS

When you want to "reformat" some of your old programs, you should know that we're not trying to give you all of the credit for changing your life. "Believing in yourself . . ." doesn't mean that you believe in nothing else.

Like many people, I grew up in a very religious family. It was always expected of me that I would grow up to work in the church. (I can only hope that the work I do now, though it is not speaking from a pulpit, will suffice.)

If you trust in your faith, you want to be very careful about what kinds of new programs you give yourself. The kind of Self-Talk we are talking about here is designed to work *with* your spiritual beliefs.

By giving ourselves the right, new, and more positive

messages of Self-Talk, we are never, in any way, trying to be humanistic, or trying to take credit away from the source of our faith.

That is, when you listen to a Self-Talk tape, as an example, you are not saying, "I am incredible . . . and I am doing this all by *myself.*"

Instead, you may even choose to begin each Self-Talk program by adding the words, "Through my *faith* . . . I choose to do the following . . ." and then continue listening to the tape or using the script.

If you would like to read some of our earliest forms of Self-Talk, reread Psalms, perhaps the greatest Self-Talk that has ever been written. Or reread Proverbs.

The right Self-Talk is never designed to compete with your faith. The *right* Self-Talk can build your faith, as it has for many others. It is designed to go hand in hand with prayer, faith, and positive belief.

With that in mind, here is another script of Self-Talk that will give you more of the right kinds of programs—to help you reach your goals each day as an Amway Distributor.

Imagine starting your day, every day, with *this* kind of Self-Talk to get you started!

SPECIAL AMWAY DISTRIBUTOR
SELF-TALK SCRIPT #5:

"I CAN DO THIS—AND I KNOW I CAN!"

I can do this, and I know I can. I've got what it takes—and I prove it every day.

I choose to be special, unique, and filled with belief.

I have faith. I know I can do this—I know I can win!

I have made the decision to create my success. I plan it, I work at it, and I BELIEVE in it.

I choose to be successful—as an individual, as a partner, and as a member of my team!

I have made the decision to win—and nothing can stop me now!

I refuse to let anything get me down. I keep my attitude "up," and I keep going for it!

I choose to have a positive, healthy attitude about my business and my success.

My attitude is my choice, and I choose to feel great, believe in myself, follow the plan, and go for my goals!

I have faith! I believe in myself, I believe in the work I am doing, and I believe in the future I am creating for my family and myself. I have faith!

I have made the decision to make my business work right! I am successful, and so is my business.

I really like the future I am creating for myself, and for the people I care about most.

I care about my business, and it shows. My business takes care of me—because I take care of my business.

I do everything I need to do to make my Amway business succeed.

I enjoy working at my business—every day—and I enjoy every positive blessing my business brings to my life.

I have chosen to win—right now, and every day. I have faith. I believe. And I succeed!

I am a winner—and I am winning right now!

I CAN DO THIS . . . AND I KNOW I CAN!

That is the kind of Self-Talk that not only helps you change your programs and create your success—that is the kind of Self-Talk that builds faith, belief, and self-esteem. The more you listen to it, or practice it, the more successful and healthy your own self-esteem will become.

YOUR *SELF-ESTEEM* IS YOUR *FUTURE*

Your programs of self-esteem (everything you believe about yourself) determine everything you do. Everything you think, everything you say, and every action you take, right down to the smallest detail—all of that is governed by the self-esteem programs you carry with you right now.

Nothing will affect your success as an Amway Distributor more than your self-esteem. That's good news! Because your self-esteem is also something you can *change.*

Always remember, you can do this—and you know you can!

Part IV
Heading For The Stars

*"As an Amway Distributor,
you're one of the most important
professionals there is.*

*If you want to make sure you
stay on track,
give yourself a program checkup.
Then, tomorrow, do it again.*

*You, and your Amway business,
are worth it."*

Chapter Fourteen
Your Daily Program Checklist

One of the benefits of working in the field of human behavior is that you eventually learn some great truths about what makes good lives work well. You learn, as I have, that some motivational ideas sound great, but do little, while other ideas change lives in incredible ways.

The tool I share with you now is easy to use, even on an everyday basis, but it can be literally life-changing in its results. It always seems to be the simplest ideas that work the best. And yet, they are the first to be ignored. They sound *so* simple—how could they possibly change your life?

If you were to do this one exercise, daily at first, and then weekly or even occasionally thereafter, for even the next three or four years, I believe you would surpass everyone around you at your level in Amway. I'm sure that if you followed this advice, you would also reach every Amway goal, and personal goal, that you set.

WHAT IS THE SECRET THAT
PROFESSIONALS HAVE LEARNED?

After years of intensive training, an astronaut, before he is launched into space to begin his journey into the heavens, learns to do one thing better than any other single thing he will do. It is such a simple thing that one would almost wonder why it took so many years, and so much practice, to get good at doing it.

If you learned this same skill, you would be more effective and even more successful. Yet this skill is not taught in school, or even suggested in most careers. It's a skill that is taught, understood, and used in only the most serious and vital jobs.

Astronauts do it before they would ever think of leaving the earth. Pilots do it before every flight. Doctors do it before and after every operation they undertake. Builders do it before they lay the first brick of construction. And divers do it before they take their first step into the water beneath them.

In each of these cases, the people are trained to do one thing that is vital to their success. And in each of these cases, the people involved are preparing themselves to succeed.

What is it that all of these highly successful people do? They perform one, simple, exceptionally important task. They fill out a *checklist*.

YOUR OWN SUCCESS IS JUST AS IMPORTANT

When was someone's flight into space more important that

180

your flight into your future? When was a doctor's physical exam more important than your own examination of where you stand and what you're doing now?

When was a builder's set of plans more important than the plans you have outlined for your own *life*? When was a diver's pre-dive checklist more important than your own review of your preparedness to step into the unknown, find the treasure, and come out on top?

Imagine having your own checklist—one that you could fill out every day, or every time you took a step that could affect your future (which is exactly what you do every day).

What you're doing for yourself, and for everyone you meet and sponsor, is just as important as any of the checklist-trained professionals I have just mentioned. Actually, you are *more* important than they are. *They* might be stepping into the unknown; *you* are changing the world.

THE DAILY CHECKLIST—A PATTERN FOR YOUR NEW PROGRAMS TO FOLLOW

The following checklist is designed to help you evaluate what your most important programs are right now, and work with you to build and reinforce your positive *new* programs.

Read through the checklist now, just to familiarize yourself with the points it covers. After that, you have my permission to make as many copies of the checklist as you want. The more times you review the items on the list, the more focus, energy, determination, and action programs you will build.

Along with each of the items on the list, I've included a

brief example of the *right* kind of Self-Talk programs to help you create a *pattern* for your own new programs to follow, each time you use the checklist.

My Daily Program Checklist

Complete this checklist once each day for the next three to four weeks. Thereafter read through the checklist again, at least once each week. Each time you go through the list of questions, practice answering them using your new Self-Talk. The more often you do this, the stronger your new programs will become.

❏ **Checklist Question #1:**
   Do I *believe* in myself?

(Example:)
   I choose to *really* believe in myself! I have an unstoppable faith in my dream, and I believe completely in its achievement. My dream is important. My dream is worthwhile, and positive, and good, and I deserve to achieve it. So I make the positive choice to believe in myself completely, without doubt or hesitation at any time. I have absolute, complete faith in myself and in my dream.

❏ **Checklist Question # 2:**
   How is my *energy*?

   I make sure that I feel incredible, energetic, fit, and on top of the world. I know my dream takes active energy, so I make the choice to keep myself in good shape physically and mentally. I make sure that I have all the energy I need to get the job done.

☐ **Checklist Question # 3:**
How are my *attitude* and my *enthusiasm*?

I know that, along with the plan, my own *attitude* is the most important part of my success with Amway. So I make sure that my attitude is so upbeat and positive that my success is guaranteed. With my attitude, I make *every* day an incredible day.

☐ **Checklist Question # 4:**
How well am I *communicating* my faith in Amway, to my family and to others, today?

I choose to be a great husband (or wife), parent, counselor, motivator, teacher, and friend. As an Amway Distributor, I'm helping many people—in many areas of their lives. So I "tell the story," with my words, with my actions, and by the positive example I set. I enjoy sharing the many rewards from my successful Amway business with those I love—and because of Amway, I am closer to my family every day.

☐ **Checklist Question # 5:**
How well am I *working the plan?*

I choose to follow the plan *to the letter*. It *works,* so I follow it, exactly. No exceptions.

❏ Checklist Question # 6:
How well am I doing at *prospecting*?

I make prospecting one of the most positive activities of my life. I look forward to *sharing the dream* with everyone I meet. So that's exactly what I have made the decision to do. And I act on that decision every day.

❏ Checklist Question # 7:
How well am I doing at *showing* the plan?

I really like showing the plan, and my enthusiasm shows. I work to make sure my presentation skills are strong, as well as my belief. Because I work the plan myself, I show the plan often.

❏ Checklist Question # 8:
Am I using the right *Self-Talk* to help me be successful?

I make sure I've got the right mental programs—and I refuse to let any old or negative programs get in my way. So I make Self-Talk an important part of my life. I am learning an entire new vocabulary of the kind of Self-Talk that creates strong new programs of success in every part of my life. And each time I read this checklist, my new Self-Talk gets even stronger.

❏ Checklist Question #9:
Am I *doing everything I can do* to reach my goals?

I have made the decision to make success as an Amway Distributor a full-time occupation—and I give it the attention it deserves. My Amway career will take good care of me, so I take good care of it. I take advantage of every tool and skill Amway offers me, and I do everything I need to do, when I need to do it. That means right now. Today.

❏ Checklist Question #10:
How is my *faith*?

My spiritual faith *can* work miracles in my life. I choose to have the kind of faith that guides me, strengthens me, and uplifts me on each step of my journey. I live by my faith, and it is always with me. I choose to spend my time with others who have strong spiritual values, and together, we become stronger than ever.

❏ Checklist Question #11:
Have I *scheduled* attending my next Amway seminar or weekend event?

I make the time to attend every teaching, sharing opportunity that Amway provides to me. I make Amway meetings and events my *number one priority*. Attending Amway functions doesn't *take* time—it adds immeasurably to my business and to my life.

❏ Checklist Question #12:
What *action* can I take right now, today—to help me move *forward* in my business and in my life?

I work the plan. I live it. I make it mine. I dream the dream. I visualize it; I walk around in it; I touch it; *I give it life*. I choose to be successful, so I take action right now, today, to help me reach my personal and professional goals. Today and every day, *I work the plan!*

What a profound impact that simple but powerful checklist process can have on your life! You can almost *feel* the new programs start to take over as you read and practice your *new* Self-Talk responses.

The checklist is simple, but it builds your new programs in two very effective ways: by changing your actions—and your *results*—right now, and by helping you build long-term *programs* of success, day by day.

On the next page, I have included that same checklist again, in its abbreviated form, for you to copy and carry with you. Again, as you read over the checklist, answer each question with the Self-Talk response you would *most* like to program into your own personal, mental computer.

My Daily Program Checklist

☐ 1. Do I *believe* in myself?

☐ 2. How is my *energy*?

☐ 3. How are my *attitude* and my *enthusiasm*?

☐ 4. How well am I *communicating* my faith in Amway, to my family and to others, today?

☐ 5. How well am I *working the plan*?

☐ 6. How well am I doing at *prospecting*?

☐ 7. How well am I doing at *showing* the plan?

☐ 8. Am I using the right *Self-Talk* to help me be successful?

☐ 9. Am I doing everything I can do to reach my goals?

☐ 10. How is my *faith*?

☐ 11. Have I scheduled *attending* my next Amway function or weekend event?

☐ 12. What *action* can I take right now, today—to help me move *forward* in my business and in my life?

YOU, AND YOUR BUSINESS, ARE WORTH IT

How *is* your self-belief? Do you have the energy and enthusiasm you need to get the job done? Is your attitude always positive? Do you attract *quality* people to you? Do you follow the plan down to the last detail? Do you spend the time you should, prospecting and showing the plan? Have you made plans to attend the next Amway weekend function, yet? Are you doing everything you can do to work the plan and reach your goals, both in your business and in the rest of your life?

When you ask yourself those questions, the answers you give should reflect the *choices* you choose to make. Each time you ask, and each time you answer, you are *programming in* the results you want to create. Go over this checklist as often as you can; think about it, discuss it with your family and your sponsor, and invest the time it takes to build these strong new programs of success.

You, and your Amway business, are worth it.

"If there were two of you,
and one of you chose
to practice and reinforce
the good ideas
you have learned,
but the other "you" didn't—

Which of the two of you
would you vote for
to succeed?"

Chapter Fifteen
Review, Repeat, And *Reinforce*

What is the answer, then? What is the secret to winning in this incredible world of network marketing? You can be certain of this: the answer to success in this business is not *out there* somewhere—the answer is *in here*. Right *here*, *inside* of you, in the part of you that is reading these words right now.

So much has been written about self-help and personal motivation, and winning in life. You'd think the whole world would have it figured out by now. And yet, it is easy to miss the truth. Instead of finding the answer, most of the world just goes on getting by, achieving little, and thinking that's just the way it has to be—*when it doesn't have to be that way at all!*

But you're different. You know better, and you have at least some of the answers figured out. And you, if you keep working at it, are going to reach all of those kinds of successes that the *rest* of the world only dreams about.

How do you know? You've already passed the test. You have already shown the signs that say, "*I*, for one, would like to live at my *best*." If that were not true, you would not be reading these words right now, and you would not have gotten interested in this business in the first place. After all, this is a business for people who want to achieve.

That means you're in the right place. You've chosen the right organization, you've got all of the right tools, the opportunity is in front of you, and you're ready to move forward.

NOW, WHAT DO YOU *REALLY* DO NEXT?

Now, watch what happens next, very closely. Look at yourself, but also observe the people *around* you—those who are also in network marketing, or who are about to be.

This is where the winners and the *also-rans* line up in two *separate* groups. This is when those who are actually going to *win* will do something *different* from all the others.

This is when the winners *prepare* to win.

Up to this point, most things have been equal. That is, everyone in the business, at least to some extent, *wants* to win. Also, everyone in the business, at least in your organization, has the same tools and the same opportunity.

But it is at this moment that *some* of them—but not all of them—will step into the winner's circle—the group of those who are about to arm themselves for absolute, unconditional success. They've got all of the *external* support they need to become successful—but these people aren't stopping there.

Now, the ones who are *really* going to win, make sure they've got the *internal* support they need to win—they get their *minds* ready for success.

These are the ones who know that *real* success has to come from within. If you can train your *body* to succeed, doesn't it make sense that it is just as important to train your *mind* to succeed as well?

Every Olympic gold-medal winner knows the truth about training your mind. Like an athlete who wants to win, every Amway Distributor who wants to be successful has a *responsibility*—both to himself and to his organization—to build and prepare his mind in the right way. Build your mind, and you will build your business.

Those who win, in *this* business especially—*prepare their minds to succeed!*

They get their mental conditioning in shape; they exercise it every day. They condition, they practice, they perfect their performance, and they win.

A PROGRAM OF *PRACTICE* TO *GET* YOU IN SHAPE—AND *KEEP* YOU IN SHAPE

But how do you prepare? What should you do next, if you really want to make this work?

What truly helps—and what doesn't?

I suppose you could spend an hour in front of the mirror

each morning practicing short-term affirmations and positive thinking. But even though doing that might motivate you for the moment, and make you feel better, research has shown that changing neurological pathways in the brain takes a lot more than that.

You could try self-hypnosis (which I do *not* recommend) or you could try to silently psych your way to success by listening to "subliminal" messages (which do not—neurologically, or in *any* way—actually reach your subconscious mind).

Or you could tackle the job of reading a dozen books on programming. You could also read books on time management, personal relationships, overcoming limitations, setting goals, and building self-esteem. You could do all that, and a lot more.

But I have a solution that I believe will make the next step easier for you than all that. Keep reading the books and listening to the tapes your leaders are recommending to you, but meanwhile, there are some important things you can do that will help.

To begin with, let's go to the basics of what we're learning here, and put those basics into a simple *practice plan* that you can use any time, any day.

The goal is to set yourself up to succeed—*really* succeed—as an Amway Distributor, and to give yourself the same kind of success with your family, your home, your financial security, and the freedom to do what you choose.

And we're not talking here about some form of wishful thinking, or *hoping* it works. We're talking about the actual, practical, fundamental steps we now know it takes to create the attitudes and the actions you need to succeed.

You know from the ideas and concepts we've covered so far

that none of this is difficult. In fact, following the steps that I'm suggesting to you takes little time and little energy. More than anything else, it will take your wanting to *win*, and your *choice* to make your business *work*.

THE MORE YOU *REVIEW* IT, *REPEAT* IT, AND *REINFORCE* IT, THE BETTER IT WILL WORK

It makes sense that if programming works because of repetition and reinforcement, the first step you should take is to reinforce the specific ideas we're covering, so you learn them and *take them with you*.

You could just finish reading this book, put it down, and never pick it up again. If you did that, you would receive some value, but a few hours of reading, without reinforcing what you have read, will do little more than give you some awareness, but no real *practice*—or *programming*—to back it up.

To make sure they're getting everything possible from a book, many people reread certain chapters, or even highlight and go back over sections of the book, again and again. I often recommend doing that, and it works, but it can also take a lot of time.

So if you want to get the full benefit from the information we're covering, the following exercise entitled *"Review, Repeat, & Reinforce,"* will help. It will make it easy for you to rapidly review the basics, and go right to the area you want to work on next.

194

REVIEW, REPEAT, & *REINFORCE*

Action Step #1:
Recognize how important you and your organization really are.

You ARE special. So is your organization. You are changing your life, and you are changing the world.

Review that message *frequently!* Just before you show the plan the next time, go back to this page and read those words once or twice out loud or to yourself. If I were there at that moment, I would tell you very clearly how important your next presentation is—and I would let you know your value, your importance, and your ability to get the job done.

You can also do that yourself. Read the words. And then read them again.

Action Step #2:
Photocopy the framed quote from page 10 of this book.

Hang it on the wall in front of your desk, and read it often. When you read it, remember—it is written about *you*.

Action Step #3:
Photocopy and place other key "programming quotes" where you will read them often.

Reread all of the quote pages from the book, select the ones you want to be reminded of, or the ones you need to work on most, photocopy them, and put them where you will see them most *often.*

There is an important reason for using the framed quotes in the way I am suggesting. Those quotes are included for a purpose. The messages contained in them are positive, realistic, and important *programs.* They are designed to be.

Each time you read one of them, you are giving yourself another self-message—another program. Strong programming requires repetition—a lot of it. So reading the framed quotes won't change all of your program pathways, of course; they're not intended to.

But they are designed to *set the stage,* to make the *announcement* to the *rest* of your programming: that *these* are the kinds of messages you now *choose* to have in your computer.

Surrounding yourself with success doesn't just mean surrounding yourself with the friends or associates you choose. It means literally surrounding yourself with the right *programs*—in *every* way—with every message you get.

Action Step #4:
Learn, review, and practice the Nine Key Virtues of successful network marketing.

Read the list of nine essential virtues for your network marketing business at *least* once each week. Photocopy the list (which I have reproduced for you here); put it on the wall, or carry a copy in your planner.

Reading the list will do more than just serve as a reminder; every time you read this list you will be *preparing* yourself with another set of self-directions.

Not only will you be reminding yourself of some of the most positive, healthy, action-oriented programs you can ever get—you will also be reminding yourself to *practice* these essential virtues for yourself.

THE NINE KEY VIRTUES OF SUCCESSFUL NETWORK MARKETING

(Read these frequently, and *consciously practice* each of them.)

1. **Key Virtue #1—***VISION*

2. **Key Virtue #2—***POSITIVE USE OF YOUR TIME*

3. **Key Virtue #3—***COMMITMENT*

4. **Key Virtue #4—***BELIEF*

5. **Key Virtue #5—***SELF-ACCEPTANCE*

6. **Key Virtue #6—***TAKING RESPONSIBILITY*
   FOR YOURSELF

7. **Key Virtue #7—***CARING ABOUT OTHERS*

8. **Key Virtue #8—***SPIRITUAL VALUES*

9. **Key Virtue #9—***POSITIVE REPROGRAMMING*

Action Step #5:
Immediately begin monitoring and editing your own Self-Talk.

Begin, right now, to change your Self-Talk at home, at work, and especially in your work as a distributor. Identify the programs that are stopping you or holding you back, and immediately begin to change them.

Action Step #6:
Read the Self-Talk scripts that are printed in the book, out loud, or silently to yourself.

The scripts that I have included in this book are not intended to be read once, and then be forgotten. Each of these scripts is designed to be read or listened to *often*—daily, if you can.

If you study the scripts carefully, you will notice that each of them targets a single important area of your life or your business. But at the same time, they create programs that deal with that subject from many different points of view. It is like looking at an object, or something you want to study, and seeing it from every side, and all the most important angles.

When you practice using a Self-Talk script of this kind that I've written for you, you are doing much more than just repeating a dozen or so phrases that sound good. You are very methodically opening a broad variety of different filing cabinets in your brain; you are working on *all* of the important programs—not just one or two of them.

What sounds like simple repetition is actually a process of *rewiring* old neural circuits in the brain. To do it right, you have to rewire all of the right circuits. And you have to repeat the new programs often enough to actually create the new circuits—the new pathways.

That's what the Self-Talk scripts are for. They're there to read, repeat, and "type in" to your computer keyboard, again and again until they become permanent, fixed, new programs in the brain.

And when you practice those specially-written scripts, you are giving yourself a strong new *pattern* for the *rest* of your own self-programming to follow. By following the scripts, you know you're going to get it right.

As you can see from reading them, any of these special Self-Talk program scripts would be great additions to your own internal network marketing "programs."

IT'S EASY ENOUGH THAT *ANYONE* CAN DO IT

It may sound a little complicated when you're talking about reprogramming from a *neurological,* brain chemistry point of view, but when you're actually *doing* it, the process is very simple and very natural. (That's how the brain was designed to get programmed in the first place.)

The secret here will be how *often*, and how *regularly*, you read or listen to the scripts.

I am often asked, "Do you have to listen to the Self-Talk programs on tape?" The answer is, no, you do not.

The next question is always, "Will you get the reprogramming job done just as well if you just read and reread the scripts by yourself?" The answer to that one is, you can, but it will take longer, and the new programs will probably not be as strong. That's not only because tapes are worded and articulated just right. It is also because tapes never get tired.

You may not feel all that bouncy in the morning, or you may not feel like giving yourself that final set of positive programs just before you go to sleep at night. But Self-Talk tapes seem to wake up before we do, and somehow, they don't go to sleep until long after our day is over.

Whether you choose to listen to Self-Talk on tape, or just read over the programming scripts I've included in the book, get in the habit of working with your new Self-Talk *at least* once or twice each day, preferably in the morning, as you start your day, and then just before you go to sleep at night.

I cannot stress enough, the importance of getting to know this kind of Self-Talk *very* well. Research is now proving that there is a *vast difference* between people who get the right programs, and the people who *don't*.

It is essential to your business, and to the rest of your life, that you get the right programs. It is easy enough to do, and the results are literally life-changing. That sounds like a big promise. *It is.*

Action Step #7:
Use the Self-Talk to train yourself to be your own best motivator.

Your *self*-motivation is always up to the programs you have at that moment. When your programs hold you back, or when they cause you to doubt, lack confidence, or even fear the unknown, you always feel better when someone peps you up, and gets you motivated again.

When you have *programs* that motivate *you*, you end up

motivating *yourself.* That doesn't mean you don't rely on outside help and encouragement; it means you get to be your own coach.

It's a great feeling to wake up, greet the day, and have your programs automatically kick in, get you to jump out of bed, and hit the ground running.

I used to do that only on Christmas morning. Now I do it because I've added some programs that make me feel *the same way* the *rest* of the time as well.

Almost any of the Self-Talk scripts that I wrote for you in this book will help to get you motivated. Whether you choose to read them out loud or to yourself, or to listen to them, I recommend using all of the scripts I've included here to keep your motivation and your enthusiasm at their highest levels.

When you use the scripts, you will not only do better; you will be giving yourself some incredible new programs that will become *permanent* if you keep using them. My advice is, keep using them.

Action Step #8:
Decide what kind of distributor you want to be, and *create* **that style, and that business.**

Earlier I identified ten different distributor "types." You can identify almost anyone you know as fitting into one or more of these types. Some of the types clearly work better than others.

The purpose of learning to recognize these ten different styles is to give you the opportunity to make an actual *choice* about the *kind* of businessperson you would most like to be. People who *own* their own business get to decide how they want to *run* their business.

And yet, most of the distributors who fit into these categories usually don't even know that they have adopted a style that they are now following—for better or for worse.

When I discussed them, I referred to these distributor styles as "snapshots," or pictures of who those distributors are, and how they manage their businesses.

The more you recognize these styles, and the more you make clear, firm style decisions for yourself and for your own business, the better you'll get at adopting a style and a professional identity that work.

The ten styles I identified and discussed are:

Style #1—The Stealth Distributor
Style #2—The Doubting Thomas
Style #3—The Procrastinator
Style #4—The No-Direction Dynamo
Style #5—The Overnight Success
Style #6—The Silent Partner
Style #7—The Team Player
Style #8—The Plan Follower
Style #9—The Positive Dreamer
Style #10—The Starbound Distributor

Sit down together with your partner, your spouse, or your family, and talk this one over.

Decide which of the characteristics of those distributor types you want to build your business on.

Read Chapter Ten again, and decide which kind of business you want to own: which characteristics you want to adopt—or get rid of.

Be specific in your planning. Ask yourself the right kind of questions:

If you want to be a "Team Player," "Follow The Plan," "Dream Positively," and set your sights on being "The Starbound Success," *what do you really have to do?*

How should you conduct your business? What kinds of plans should you write down and work on? How will this affect everything else you do?

Small and large companies, like your local bank, or AT&T, or a home builder, or IBM, or your printer, or Microsoft, or any other successful company, all have meetings and make decisions like that. Shouldn't you do the same?

The purpose of identifying and showing you these ten distributor types is to give you an insight into how you might like to structure, identify, and manage your own business.

Once you recognize that you are in control of the style, attitudes, and direction of your own business, you know what to do next. Get specific. Make your choice—and act on it.

Action Step #9:
Make the decision to get past any fear you might have about yourself, or about this business.

This Action Step doesn't ask you to *never* fear anything again. It just suggests that you go ahead anyway.

For a moment, take a look at two people. One of them is afraid, and he lives, for the most part, in the shadows of his life. You might even imagine that you can't see this person too clearly. He's back there somewhere, in the shadows. Either he likes it there, or he's just afraid to come out.

Now look at the other person in this example. This one loves the sunlight. He is out in the open—and he lives his life and runs his business the same way. He loves to live! He's going for it!

The difference between these two people is not in their

ability to deal with fear; it is in their desire to move forward—and to never let life, or a life-changing *opportunity*, pass them by.

So instead of thinking, "Can I do this?" or "What will someone think?" or "What if it won't work?" you move forward, *immediately*—and you focus instead on *making* it work.

If you want to get rid of fear, focus on your goal. And then plan for it, prepare for it, work on it, talk about it, believe in it, and then work on it some more. When you are busy *focusing on the goal*, you are too busy to worry about the fear.

Also keep in mind that most of the fears that affect you and your business are the *unconscious* kind—the kind that stop you from doing something, without you even having to think about it.

Those fears—all of them—are old negative programs in the brain. And you know what to do about those.

Action Step #10:
Encourage your family to encourage *you*. Go past all negatives. And think for yourself.

I wonder how fast your organization would grow if everyone in it got total support at home.

Negative attitudes and ungrounded opinions can come from husbands, wives, parents, parents-in-law, sons and daughters, best friends, casual friends, bosses, and even uninformed media.

Work diligently to persuade, in a positive way, the ones at home. Ignore all the rest.

If you do not have to deal with this problem, you're fortunate. You can put your time and energies into building your business.

But if you do have someone in your home, or a close family member, who makes a point of wishing *you* would do what *they* want you to do, ask them to read the letter I wrote for them. And read it again yourself, along with rereading one or two of the Self-Talk scripts anytime this comes up.

The most important thing is that *you* keep going.

Action Step #11:
Start *immediately* focusing on your self-esteem. Practice building it—*consciously*. Set a goal that tells you how strong and positive you want your self-esteem to be. Then reach that goal.

Your self-esteem, whatever it is now, may have been *formed* by accident—but it will not *improve* by accident. You have to change it yourself.

To get very specific in your goal to build your self-esteem, it will help to ask yourself the following questions. These same questions will also make an excellent review list for you to reread now and then to check your progress on how well you're doing:

How is your self-esteem right now?
Do you see yourself as being a natural winner?
Is this business easy for you?
Do you have a lot of enthusiasm for what you're doing?
Are you willing to work hard for what you want?
Do you let other people stop you?
Do you know what you want?
Are you a person who sets long-term goals?
Do you reach your goals?
Do you have a positive attitude?
Are you a good communicator?

Do you listen when someone else is talking?

Do you express yourself well?

Do you argue?

If you argue, what do you argue about?

How is your posture?

How do you hold your head most of the time?

What things interest you most?

Who are the people you most respect?

Why do you respect them?

Are you organized?

Do you have your life under control?

Do you believe you can make a significant, positive difference in your own future?

Do you believe you can make a significant, positive difference in other people's lives?

How do you feel about your age?

Are you the kind of person who can start something and follow it through?

How is your self-belief?

Are you a good team player, and do you work well with other people?

Are you a leader?

Are you good at following a plan?

Do you believe that you have the ability to be wealthy, professionally independent, happy, and successful?

There could be a hundred more questions, just like those, on that list—but those few examples will give you the idea.

Notice that not one of those questions asked you whether you *liked* yourself. Self-esteem really isn't just about liking or loving yourself; self-esteem is the *whole picture* of who you think you are—*everything* about you.

Those questions, and more like them, will help you find out how you would actually *like* your self-esteem to *be*. The process here is to read through the list as you just did. But now, take any one of the questions and restate it. Let's take the question, *"Do you have your life under control?"* as an example.

This time when you read it, however, change it slightly. This time, ask the question, "Do I *choose* to have my life under control?"

Other examples would be restated to read, "Do I *choose* to be a good communicator," "Do I *choose* to let obstacles or problems stop me," or "Do I *choose* to be good at following a plan?" etc.

When you set a goal to improve your self-esteem, you have to first begin by knowing what that "better" self-esteem would look like. The steps are:

a. Make the choices that tell you how you want your self-esteem to be.

b. Write those choices down on paper, such as *"I choose to be a good communicator."* Start with only a dozen or so of these choices. Then add more later.

c. Next, read your list of self-esteem choices every time you have a life-planning meeting, or on a regular schedule that you set.

You will notice, when you read your list of self-esteem choices, that they look very much like Self-Talk. They *are* Self-Talk. Yours. Practice them in exactly the same way.

Action Step #12:
Photocopy your Daily Program Checklist, and read it and review it faithfully.

I recommend that you make a lot of copies of your checklist (from Chapter 14) and actually put a *check mark* in the boxes as you answer each of the questions.

You're very fortunate. Checklists don't work well for people in many other businesses, only because they have no clear-cut *plan* to *follow*. How can you stay *on track* when you don't know where the track *is*?

But you are in a business that was built on a plan; you have a track you cannot miss.

Use the checklist. Answer each one of the questions. Look for every improvement you can put into practice that will help make your business more successful.

That, also, is not difficult. That is what winners *do*.

IF THERE WERE *TWO* OF YOU,
WHICH ONE WOULD YOU VOTE FOR?

If there were *two* of you, and one of you chose to implement the action steps we've just reviewed in this chapter, but the other "you" decided to just put the book away and maybe reread it at some time or other, which one of you would you vote for to succeed—to go *Diamond*?

Reviewing these twelve Action Steps frequently will help you reinforce all of the key ideas and tools that are found throughout this book.

Using this chapter in that way will not only help you keep

the ideas and concepts fresh in your mind; it will help you begin applying the ideas *immediately*, in an effective and organized way.

When you practice these concepts, and make them a part of your business—and everything else that's important to you—you create more quality and value in your life, in your family's life, and in everything you touch.

Now let's see if we can turn what you touch into gold.

Or diamonds.

"If you truly want to be
one of those Diamonds in your sky,
you can be.

You have the <u>organization</u>.
You have the <u>tools</u>.
You have the <u>time</u>.
You have the <u>support</u>.
You have the <u>ability</u> to get there.

Don't ever let anyone
tell you anything less.

<u>You can do this</u>—
and you know you can!"

Chapter Sixteen
Believing In Incredible *You*!

A number of years ago I wrote what would turn out to be the most popular Self-Talk script I had ever written. It was entitled *"Believing In Incredible You!"* and it was different from all the other program scripts I had written. "If I could write just one, final Self-Talk script," I had thought, "what would it be?"

As it turned out, that script somehow spoke to everyone who had ever wanted to make something out of his or her life. Out of several hundred published Self-Talk scripts, to this day, that one script has been my most requested, most read, and most listened-to Self-Talk program.

But now it's time to improve upon the best. Though many Amway Distributors count that Self-Talk program among their favorites, I have been asked again and again to write that *same* kind of Self-Talk, but just for them.

You'll notice that *this* special script is written in "second person," from the *outside* coach, to the *inside* you. (It is also recorded that way, which is why it becomes such a strong motivational tool even while it is creating new programs.)

Read this one, out loud if you can, to yourself—and watch what begins to happen to your picture of yourself, right now. Bear in mind that it can sometimes feel a bit strange or uncomfortable to be "told" so many positive things about yourself all at once; most people aren't used to it. If that happens, it's perfectly all right for you to feel that way. Don't worry; with repeated use, you'll soon get used to hearing the truth—about *you*.

Here, then, is the new *"Believing In Incredible You!"* but this time, it's just for you.

SPECIAL AMWAY DISTRIBUTOR
SELF-TALK SCRIPT #6

"BELIEVING IN INCREDIBLE YOU!—
FOR AMWAY"

You ARE incredible! And you know who I'm talking about!

You've got everything you need to achieve, and nothing is going to stop you now. You've got talent, skills, and ability. You've got talents and skills you don't even know about yet!

You've got the stuff to see you through. You've got positive ambition, courage, determination, and the kind of attitude and fortitude that get you started, and never let you stop until the job is done!

You believe in yourself, you believe in your organization, you believe in Amway, and you believe in the incredible future you are creating in your life.

You have power! You have drive! You have stamina, and you have the strength to succeed. You create strong, positive energy in your life, and in the lives of everyone around you.

You keep yourself fit, active, physically in shape, energetic, filled with enthusiasm, and going for it. You take care of yourself at all times, and in everything you do.

You make sure your mind is clear, bright, alert, active, and healthy, and always working for you in the most positive possible way.

You prepare, you practice, you prospect, you show the plan, and YOU produce! You choose to succeed, so you stay with it, every opportunity, every day, every level, every step of the way!

You have faith, courage, and conviction. You know you can do it, and you prove it every day!

You are committed to your business, and you are committed to your goal. You have made a contract with yourself to succeed!

You have focus! You have a plan! You are organized! You are in control of your life, your business, and your success. So you set your sights, stay on target, restate your goal, and take action!

You are special, unique, and destined to succeed. You have values that never let you down! You care about people, and people care about you. You help others succeed in their lives, and through your efforts, you are doing your part to change the world.

You are an exceptional human being. You choose to live your life with honor, truth, values, faith, action, achievement, joy, and belief.

You are happy, full of life, and filled with spirit! Today especially! Right now, you hear the voice of that undefeatable spirit within you! You ARE special. You ARE blessed, and you carry that blessing with you into everything you say and do—today, and tomorrow, and every day.

It is your time; this is your place. Now is the moment— today is your day! So you go for it! You show the world, right now, what you CAN do—just because you choose to say YES. You choose to make your life, and your business, work in the most incredible, positive, way—right now, TODAY!

If you have ever had any doubts about yourself in the past, today is a good day to put every doubt, worry, or disbelief aside. You've got what it takes, and nothing can defeat your determination to succeed.

You hold your head high. You set your sights. You keep your balance. You don't hesitate. You don't hold back. You step forward, and you win!

Think what you can do today! Think what joy, what

214

achievement, what good, what success, you can create.

So right now you take a deep breath. You see yourself standing taller than ever, and you say YES to yourself, and YES to your success!

You ARE INCREDIBLE! And today, is a great day to prove it!

It is time to believe in you—*incredible you!* It's time to make the decision to make your business—and the rest of your life—everything it can possibly be.

Those aren't the empty words of wishful thinking or momentary motivation. What you do now is exceptionally important. Your decision to take action, get busy, work the plan, and create the freedom of an unlimited future, will be what sets you apart from the ordinary, and makes your future shine.

Follow the steps. Work the plan. Use the tools you've been given. Surround yourself with the support that is there for you. Attend the meetings and the functions. Spend time with your teammates, and build your own enthusiasm while you help them build theirs. Go to work immediately on your old programs; change the ones that have tried to limit you in the past—and add the ones you will take with you into your future.

And meanwhile, remind yourself that time is short, and there is a lot to do. Before you know it, you will reach that next level, and then the next, and then the next . . .

MAKING EACH MOMENT COUNT

I'd like to share a story with you, from my own life, that taught me the value of every moment I live. This story relates an incident, a blessing of sorts, that happened to me when I was very young—and it changed my life forever.

I was six years old when I had my first real birthday party. Among the relatives and friends from my church, who had been invited, was a very special old man. His name was Eli, a great-uncle of mine. I especially liked Eli because he was very wise, and he knew something about everything; but I liked him most because he was my friend, and he would always take the time to talk to me, and to explain new things to me.

It was sometime during that sixth birthday party that old uncle Eli told me he wanted to talk to me. So we went outside and sat down on the wooden bench under the pine trees that surrounded my home. It was night, and the sky was filled with a million, dazzling stars.

"How old are you now?" Eli asked as we sat there.

"I'm six years old," I said, very proudly.

"Can you snap your fingers?" Eli asked next.

"Sure I can," I answered, knowing that any six-year-old kid ought to be able to snap his fingers.

And with that I snapped my fingers, once, really loud, just to prove it.

"That's very good," Eli said. "Now, there is something important I would like you to do for me."

"Sure, if I can," I said.

"Next year at this time," Eli went on, "I want you to go outside, sometime during your seventh birthday party, and

216

look up at the stars. Then I want you to remember right now, and snap your fingers, just once. Will you do that for me?"

Even though I didn't know what Eli was telling me, or why, I liked him, and I was happy to agree, so I promised.

"If I'm able to be at your party next year, I'll go outside with you when you do that," he said. Then he continued, "And I'd like you to do the same thing on your eighth birthday, and then again on your ninth birthday, and on your tenth birthday. And then, do the same thing again on your fifteenth birthday, and then on your twentieth, and then on your twenty-fifth, and on every fifth birthday after that for as long as you can.

"Sometime during your party, take a few minutes and go outside by yourself, and look up at the stars, and snap your fingers, just once. Will you do that for me?" he asked.

I promised Eli that I would, even though I still couldn't figure out why he was asking me to do that. But I knew he was very smart, and he was my friend, so I promised.

Then Eli said, "Let me hear you snap your fingers again." So once again, I proudly snapped my fingers, as loud as I could. "That's good," Eli said. And then he added, " . . . By the way, did you notice that between the time you snapped your fingers just now, and when you snapped your fingers the first time, a few minutes ago, *it seemed like no time at all passed* between those two times you snapped your fingers?"

I partly understood what Eli meant, but not completely. And it wasn't until a year later, when I was seven, that I finally figured it out. Old uncle Eli couldn't come to my birthday party that year. He had gone to sleep one night during the summer, and never woke up again.

But I remembered the promise I had made to him, so during my seventh birthday party I went outside all by myself, and sat on the wooden bench under the pine trees, and looked up at the night sky that was filled with a million stars. And I thought of Eli, and I snapped my fingers just once.

It was in that *moment* that I realized what Eli had been trying to tell me: It seemed as though not a single moment had passed between the *first* time I had snapped my fingers a year before, and the time I snapped my fingers *now*. In a single instant of time, *an entire year* had gone by!

And so I did the same thing again on my eighth birthday, and on my ninth and tenth, and then again on my fifteenth, and twentieth and twenty-fifth, and every fifth birthday thereafter. Sometime, during my party, I would excuse myself for a few minutes, go outside all alone, and wherever I was, I would look up at the stars, think of Eli, and snap my fingers just once.

Not long ago I celebrated my fiftieth birthday. And as I stood out under the stars that night, and thought about all the years that had passed between that first finger-snap so many years ago, and now—I realized that I had journeyed from the boy to the man in just a few, brief "clicks" in time.

Soon, on my fifty-fifth birthday, I will snap my fingers under those stars again, and then again on my sixtieth birthday, and my sixty-fifth, and my seventieth, and every fifth year thereafter . . . for as long as I can. And each time I do, I will know that it is what I have done *between those clicks* that *counts*.

A LESSON THAT LIVES ON

A few years ago, I was alone on my birthday, and I was

hoping my son Tony would call. He was grown, and had a family of his own. But it was my birthday, and I hoped he would remember.

The evening got later and later, and I was beginning to wonder if I would have much of a birthday at all. I was about to give up hope, when finally the telephone rang. I picked up the receiver and said, "Hello," expecting to hear my son's voice on the other end of the line. But there was nothing but silence.

I said *"Hello,"* again—but still I heard nothing.

And then, finally, I heard it, and in that moment my spirits lifted to the sky. What I heard was the clear and unmistakable sound of a *finger-snap*!

It was my son, sending a message to me across the miles and across the years, reminding me he had not forgotten.

On another night, not long ago, on my grandson Anthony's sixth birthday, my son Tony took young Anthony outside to talk with him alone. And while father and son sat there together, under the stars, and talked about life, and about being six years old, my son said to Anthony, "How old are you?"

"I'm six years old," little Anthony said, very proudly.

And then my son looked up at the stars and smiled, remembering, and said to his own son, "There's something I'd like you to do for me. *I'd like you to snap your fingers, just once."*

IT'S WHAT YOU DO *NOW* THAT COUNTS

It is *true. It is what you do between those few, brief,*

finger-snaps of life that counts. It is what you do now, and every day that follows, that will make the difference.

If you truly want to be one of those diamonds in your sky, you can be.

You have the *organization.*

You have the *tools.*

You have the *time.*

You have the *support.*

And you have the *ability* to get there.

Don't ever let anyone tell you anything less. *You can do this,* and you know you can!

Right now, pause for a moment. Take a deep breath, and relax. Feel good about yourself.

And then I would ask you to do just one more thing: Pause for just one more moment. Think about your *incredible, unlimited* future. See yourself living the life of your dreams. And then, *right now . . . snap your fingers, just once.*

You *are* changing the world.

I wish you well.

To reach Dr. Helmstetter, contact:
Self-Talk Information Services
P.O. Box 65659
Tucson, AZ 85728

For information on currently available Self-Talk Cassettes, including a special set of Self-Talk Cassettes for Amway Distributors, featuring the Self-Talk scripts which are included in this book, you may contact the publisher of Self-Talk Cassettes directly at 1-800-982-8196.

To order additional copies of the book,
"Network Of Champions,"
call 1-800-982-8196.